This is a book that we highly recommend to be read by each couple prior to or during the time of marriage counseling. It is a great resource that will help couples progress through struggles they may encounter.

Wayne and Ruth Kuhns
Director, Spring of Hope Counseling Ministries
Waynesboro, Pennsylvania

I can only imagine what would happen if with both hands we would grasp hold of the message of this book and hold it close to our hearts…. It will change your life…

—Benjamin R. Musser
A Loving Father

This book is encouraging and life-giving

—Ann Chilcote
Co-Pastor of My Father's House Ministries

Ecstasy of Love

Reaching New Levels of Intimacy As You Redefine ONENESS

STEPHANIE GOSSERT

stephaniegossert@gmail.com.

Published in Collaboration with IONgdw | www.iongdw.com
Cover and Book Design by Jeffrey M. Hall | www.iongdw.com

Cover and author photo by Hope Bigler | www.hopebigler.com

ISBN: 978-0-9910255-0-3

For Worldwide Distribution, Printed in the U.S.A.

First Printing: 2013

Dedication

Ecstasy of Love was designed for all who have a desire to experience so much more than what they have yet to see in life, love, and commitment. There is always more!

Acknowledgements

To the Creator of heaven and earth, Papa God, Jesus, Holy Spirit, You are the reason this book exists. Thank You for allowing me to be part of it. Thank You for every time you pressed me, encouraged me, and prodded me to write and believe it was You. Thank You for the angels You released to accomplish this work. It is very honoring and humbling what You chose to do in the life of a believer! This book is evidence, to me, of Your Spirit and Your interwoven tapestry of Your Body.

To Steve, my amazing husband, thank you for believing in me and committing yourself to me and our marriage. I could not have written this without you. Thank you for allowing God's Spirit to move in you! Thank you for supporting me in all my endeavors.

Shyann, Siara, Shawnee, and Sakari, what amazing daughters you are: Each one of you is a gift! Thank you for encouraging me to write! Thank you for being patient and understanding when we had to shift gears to complete this project. I am very proud of each one of you!

Thank you, Mom, you have taught me to be strong, persevere through all things, and reach for the highest! Thank you for always telling me I can do anything I want to do! Thank you, Dad and Faye, for always saying to me, "Why can't you?" Thank you for believing in me!

Thank you to all of my family for your constant love and encouragement. Thank you Aunt Blanche, you are a grandma to me and I am very grateful for your love and support! What I witnessed in your marriage is what I want to experience; it helped to give me vision. Thank you, Hope, for your awesome gift of photography.

Thank you to my family, the Body of Christ. Papa knew I would need many mentors, intercessors, and encouragers of His heart to get my sail in His winds! I am so thankful that you chose to carry His heart for me! Rhonda, though you have crossed over into the heavens, you were always one of my biggest cheerleaders. I just want to say, thank you for still cheering me on!!!!

Thank you to all of you in leadership who continually encourage and affirm me; I am honored! Thank you, Mary, for praying for my eyes to be open, teaching me to worship, and to love the Word! Thank you, Cathy, for encouraging me to go deeper and deeper in the Spirit, to trust Him inside of me. Thank you, Ben, for being the encouragement of Fire and Love behind me. Thank You, Monica, for tie-roping me into submitting the first works to an editor. Sometimes we have to be lovingly nudged to the edge of the precipice! Thank you, Jeff and Jacqueline for your help and support to complete this project! When I needed encouragement, it has *always* been there! I am truly blessed!

Endorsements and Reviews

I can only imagine what would happen if with both hands we would grasp hold of the message of this book and hold it close to our hearts.

If you need to be reminded what passion and unconditional love is and who it's for, then this book is written for you. It will change your life, your story, and the lives of everyone you touch.

Benjamin R. Musser
A Loving Father
bmusser9556@gmail.com

Ecstasy of Love is an absolute read for anyone who is struggling in marriage or who wants to experience everything God intended for marriage. Stephanie loves her heavenly Father (Papa) and writes in a style that makes you feel she is sitting with you sharing her heart and wisdom. At times you will think, *Yes, that is what I'm feeling,* or *Yes, that's what I want in my marriage.* She has included many prayers that can be helpful to you as you begin to practice the things that will help you experience marriage as God intended it to be. *Ecstasy of Love* contains both biblical truths and practical ways to apply those truths. Stephanie shares seven practical suggestions that should probably be posted throughout our homes, but more importantly, put into practice continually.

Wilbur (Buck) Besecker
Retired Pastor and Family Counselor
Waynesboro, Pennsylvania

Stephanie Gossert is a passionate daughter of God who desires the body of Christ to experience the fullness of intimacy God created for us to enjoy. Through personal testimonies and revealing God's truth, her book helps expose the world's schemes and counterfeits. The tools she provides help replace and restore purity, purpose, and passion into the marriage covenant. She focuses on God's truth and chooses to trust in Him and His promises. This mindset enables God to intervene and bring about the transformation we desire in our lives.

This book is encouraging and life-giving. It truly focuses on walking in the love of God, allowing His presence to reveal and heal. In this work, Stephanie reflects well God's heart of restoration for His people. It is a must read for all who desire to improve their relationship with God, their spouse, and others.

Ann Chilcote,
Co-Pastor, My Father's House Ministries
McConnellsburg, Pennsylvania

This book is straight from the heart of God! Today most marriage help books and marriage counseling focus so much on just fixing the problems in a marriage without ever bringing God into the discussion. As a pastor, it is hard for me to count the number of times individuals came for marriage counseling and just stated all of things that were wrong with their spouses, with the expectation of having me fix them; or worst case scenario, wanting me to give them permission to leave the marriage.

The only thing I have found that helps a marriage flourish is for the individuals to be truly growing in their personal walks with God. Through this growth, we become more like Jesus who allows us to exhibit more of His character in our lives and into our relationships such as love, patience, self-control, and selflessness. That is exactly what this book encourages. It lays out the importance of God being the foundation and the need for God's ever-increasing presence in our lives. This is not a quick fix, but a process of growing into the fullness of what God has for our marriages and families.

I truly believe that anyone who has a desire for God's presence in their marriage can begin to walk out the truths that are inspired in this book. They will see their lives and marriages transformed through the model of God's unconditional love. This book is a vital resource for anyone who is married or about to be married and desires the fullness of God in their relationship. My wife and I believe this book will challenge you wherever you are in your marriage! God has brought you and your spouse together not just to survive, but for so much greater!

Jason & Stacy Hostetter
Co-Pastors of Windward Ministries
Winfield, Pennsylvania

We have been blessed to have known Stephanie for ten years and consider her a very good friend. We have shared in ministry, worship, and prayer. If there is one thing we can say about Stephanie, she is trustworthy and she has a genuine love for others. Stephanie always seeks to maintain a healthy relationship with us no matter what the challenges.

There is no doubt that this book is written from a heart that loves. She desires others to experience the ecstasy of love that she encounters through intimacy with God and with her husband. This book is written from experience in a journey over years of seeking God. Stephanie not only sought God for answers, but walked out in very practical ways her obedience to the answers she discovered.

So, if you are struggling with relationships, this book is for you! You will be encouraged as you discover how to grow in your relationship with God and with your spouse. This is not for those who want to be satisfied with just getting along; but if you desire to experience real joy and fulfillment in your relationships, then you will find the practical experiences and lessons learned in this book helpful for your journey to ecstasy.

What we value in this book is that it is not written out of theology, doctrine, or intellect; but is written from a person's own experience of struggling to apply what God has shown her in practical ways. We have been part of over fifty marriage retreats, and we would recommend this book as a realistic answer to strengthen marriage.

Thanks, Stephanie, for sharing with us your very personal journey to ecstasy of love in your marriage. It has encouraged us in our own journey.

Rick and Peg Hostetter
Cyan Ministries, Inc.

Ecstasy of Love is a bold, honest, and truthful approach for a lasting and fulfilling covenant marriage relationship that has been developed from Stephanie's heartfelt convictions as a result of her experiences in life and her marriage. She vividly points out the necessity of taking full responsibility for *our reactions and responses* to what our spouse does or does not do for us. Our responses cannot come from an emotional reaction; rather, they must come from an intimate relationship with Papa (our Heavenly Father). We must take a look, within our own hearts, and ask God what He wants to do in our hearts because of what we have experienced in our marriage—meanwhile we are praying and believing that our spouses are allowing God to search their hearts as well.

Stephanie very clearly describes the importance, when speaking to our spouses or about our spouses to another person, that we only speak words of blessing and life. This happens when we see within our spouses the same things that God sees within them, and we speak it forth. This is the fruit that is revealed, in our life and marriage, when we consciously make choices that are in alignment with God's design for our lives.

Wayne and Ruth Kuhns
Director, Spring of Hope Counseling Ministries
Waynesboro, Pennsylvania

I have had the privilege of knowing Stephanie Gossert since she was in her early twenties and a newlywed. I have had the opportunity to watch her grow and mature from a young, married woman to a wife and mother of four beautiful and amazing daughters. Along her journey Stephanie has not just bloomed into a beautiful godly woman, she has soared! Her passion and hunger for God and oneness with Him and others is contagious. I greatly appreciate her honesty, openness to the Holy Spirit, and her burning devotion to her King. I see an anointing on her to touch, teach, and bring healing to others with her gifts. This book is a book of Truths. It is not only about oneness and ecstasy in our marriages but also about finding fullness and oneness in every aspect of our lives! Read this book with an open heart and spirit, and allow the truths therein to take you into deeper places of intimacy in your marriage and in your walk of life!

Cat Miller

www.divinehealingsounds.com

As a single woman, I am very honored to write an endorsement for *Ecstasy of Love*. Through the years I have known Stephanie, I have watched her take on the role of a sister, a mother, a friend, a mentor, and a grandmother to those God places in front of her. The greatest gift I have learned from her is to understand that people have opinions, even prophetic words, and wisdom from God, but we are ultimately responsible for our own lives. We ourselves answer to God for our decisions, no one else but ourselves! At the end of a conversation with another person we still need to have our eyes ultimately on Jesus and not that person or the situation!

She encourages in these writings the same as she has taught me and that is to look confrontation in the eyes and not to run away from it. I used to run from confrontation because I didn't know how to interact with someone else when we didn't agree. I never understood how to pray and love on that person to see them with the eyes of God, through His love, and to hear them with an open heart to work out the difference or to agree that we see things differently!

There is an incredible testimony she speaks about in this book where she is the dutiful mother and wife trying to do everything so her husband can rest. We were brought up in a decade that it was expected of mothers to do everything, because the husband works hard to provide for the family! I myself might have been just as guilty of not allowing God or my husband to help me! We live in a world that expects us to be able to do for ourselves and not to ask for help because that makes us weak! She put that expectation on herself and realized after she broke down and finally spoke to her husband that it was not an expectation he had for her! She speaks these words that I feel are very important for us to get, "That doesn't seem wrong in and of itself, yet in doing this God started showing me I was hindering Steve from becoming who God was calling him to be, as a father and as a husband. I was in the way. I was all but killing myself so he could rest, not loving myself in the process. I had put expectations on myself that weren't even real and I was enabling him to rise up in the responsibilities."

In all areas of my life, I can use this to help me empower people to walk in their destiny and not to hinder them by enabling some form of pride! Pride is deceiving and takes our eyes off of God and puts them on ourselves! Pride is sometimes false humility in believing we are to be self reliant and not reliant on God or others at times! I am encouraged and also challenged to continually press into greater ecstasy with God and hopefully experience that with my future husband!

Trina Olson

Here is a "woman after God's own heart"! Stephanie Gossert, in the few short years that she has lived life, has learned what works and what doesn't! She is a woman of great wisdom and when she speaks, we should listen! In *Ecstasy of Love*, Stephanie shares her heart in what it takes to build a marriage that will stand the test of time. She is a dear friend who exudes the love of Christ and I always feel like I've been renewed in my Spiritual walk after having spent time with her! So go ahead, read this one, experience the "Ecstasy", and rejoice with me in welcoming Stephanie into the world of great authors! I believe we will be hearing much more from her in the days ahead!

Harold E. Wildeson
President, Singing in the Barn, Inc.
Chambersburg, Pennsylvania

What an unexpected, amazing journey I was invited to travel, recently. Stephanie Gossert was in the process of writing her first book when a mutual friend thought we needed to meet for the purpose of my reading Stephanie's manuscript and offering to her, some editing feedback. This was my introduction to the name, Stephanie Gossert. Everything about this encounter was spiritually designed from beginning to end. We met in person, only once, and I began reading Stephanie's book, Ecstasy of Love. I soon discovered that Stephanie is a young lady who freely calls her God, Papa, because of her obvious love for Him, relationship with Him, and living IN HIM. We communicated for two weeks, only by computer, sharing edits, comments, and questions about her drafts. After thirty years as a middle school educator, I was accustomed to editing students' works on a regular basis; editing then, for the sole purpose of teaching writing and reading skills. What I have just experienced in my journey with Stephanie Gossert was a Godsend. Though we had come face-to-face only once, prior to beginning our working relationship, we came heart-to-heart many times in the final days of her completing the book you are now blessed to be holding. Stephanie took the passion of her heart and put it into writing to share with others what she has learned about living in ecstasy as God intended, in her marriage and her personal walk each day. As I came to know Stephanie's heart through her writing, I came to know, also, the heart of God, at a much deeper level. I have been inspired, challenged, and have found emotional healing in the very pages that also brought laughter, and sometimes, tears. Having personally experienced the devastation of divorce in my early adult years, I wish I would have had the opportunity, during that time of much confusion, to read Ecstasy of Love. Stephanie Gossert's words on each page echo the heart of God and the fullness of the life He has designed for each of us.

Jacqueline K. Perdas
A grateful child of God
Retired Middle School Educator

Contents

Forewords

ECSTASY

WHAT an interesting subject that stirs our curiosity. People love the thought of ecstasy, but many don't realize the foundation that needs to be laid for this kind of experience. I believe in order for ecstasy to exist there must first be intimacy. Intimacy develops over time with trust, commitment, love, and relationship.

When we come to know the Lord or when we find someone of the opposite sex, we are driven by a passion, and so the relationship starts. We commit to the process of finding out about what God is like or what this person is like. We begin to love what we are finding out and enjoy being in their presence. Trust begins to develop.

As a new believer or a newlywed, we have expectations of what life will be like. However, after the honeymoon, the issues of life and the unexpected sometimes shake our faith. We begin to ponder thoughts such as, *How did God let this happen?* or *I never saw this characteristic in my spouse.*

In Chapter 3, Fighting for Your Destiny, Stephanie points out the pitfalls that will destroy both our relationship with not only our spouse, but also with God. The enemy of our soul prowls around like a roaring lion seeking whom he might devour. Although he has lost his power, he seeks to destroy through suggestion, disappointment, dissatisfaction, hurts, and others—just as he did in the Garden.

One of the many things I affirm in this book is that when problems arise, take them quickly to the Father. Tell Him your concerns, disappointments, and frustrations. He is our defender and always our help in times of need. He will work for you! As long as you keep your problems to yourself, it hinders the Holy Spirit's activity in dealing with the situation. The quicker you give these issues over to Him, the less pain you will experience and the quicker you will rebound. One of the keys to intimacy with our spouses and God is first listening and then communicating back the things that you heard. The greater the communication, the more you will experience relationally.

Stephanie has a lot to share in this book. It should be read and used as a manual and a source of reference. Read this book to uncover ecstasy in your walk with God—and your spouse.

Gene Strite
Genestrite.com

Rachael and I have been friends with Stephanie Gossert for several years, and I was honored when she asked me to read her book and write a Foreword. I thoroughly enjoyed reading *Ecstasy of Love*. What a great title! In an age when bookstore shelves are filled with books about divorce and broken marriages, it was refreshing to read a book that highlights the joy and ecstasy of love that is only found in marriage. This book is a great resource for engaged couples, newlyweds, couples who have been married for years, and couples who, together, are going through a time of difficulty.

There is fresh breath and revelation wrapped up in a simple yet profound package within this book. Stephanie does a wonderful job exploring the Scriptures and seeing what the Father has to say about marriage and love, and then delivers it in a practical manner. This is so important! Not only must we understand what God is saying about love, but we need to know how to apply it to everyday life. Whether you're closer to your spouse than you've ever been, or you are fighting for your marriage, I recommend that you read this book; you will receive, be refreshed and equipped with new ammunition of love for your marriage.

I have been married to Rachael for thirteen years, and we have known each other our entire lives. When I was nine years old I told my mother that I was going to marry Rachael. We've always been best friends and we've always shared our most intimate secrets with one another. We have experienced so much together in life, before marriage and in marriage, some great victories and some real struggles. But through it all we have been together.

In John 17:3 Jesus describes eternal life as knowing God and His Son that He sent. The word that He used for know is *ginosko,* the most intimate term for knowledge in the Greek language. It is a term that could also be used to describe intimacy between a husband and a wife. Eternal life is not the point of arriving to the great awakening of understanding where it all makes sense, but the process of discovering intimately who our Father is and who is this beautiful loving Son He sent to us. Marriage is very similar in that way. Although I have known Rachael her whole life and we have been through so many seasons together, there are still things that I am discovering about her on a daily basis. This may be a story I had never heard, or something that she enjoys that I hadn't known. It might be the way she smiles at something or a dream she hadn't shared before.

After thirty years together in life and thirteen years in marriage, I am still discovering who my wife is and we are growing, together. This is the joy of marriage! The journey together! Most people tend to make a big deal of the wedding ceremony, and that's understandable it's a special day, but some of my favorite memories are the day-to-day steps that we take together, like when we didn't have money for oil to heat our house so we bought an extra blanket and cuddled up together—we were so happy! Just as with our relationship with the Father and with Jesus, marriage is not a destination but a journey. A beautiful and challenging journey!

In the beginning God created man from the dust of the earth and gave him life from his own breath (see Genesis 2:7). The original position of man was face to face with Papa God. At this point Adam was the full package, created in the image of his Father. But when God saw that Adam did not have a companion, He decided to create Eve. How did He do that? It was a different process from how He created Adam. God caused Adam to sleep and He pulled one of his ribs out and created Eve (see Genesis 2:21-24). The Bible actually says that she was taken out of Adam. Before the creation of Eve, Adam was the full representation of the image of God, but now that Eve had been taken out of him, each had characteristics of the image of their Father. Woman was taken out of man not so they could be separated, but so they could be joined together in marriage and together become one, the full representation of the image of God. God is restoring husbands and wives to the original position, face to face with God, together, in marriage.

In our ministry to women in prostitution here in Brazil, we have heard some of the most heartbreaking stories you could ever imagine. But the more heartbreaking the story the more beautiful the restoration—and we have seen much of that as well. One story is that of a young woman who we met on the streets of our city one night. She was selling her body every night, sometimes twenty times a night. As we talked with her, I noticed a man across the street who was watching us closely. I assumed he was her pimp, but after a while she told us he was her husband. My heart sank. This man was on the streets negotiating with strangers the price to have sex with his wife. I wasn't angry, or even disgusted, but completely broken thinking about what they must have gone through to reach that point. I thought of all of the hard times that Rachael and I went through and never once did we come even close to that level of brokenness.

We began walking with the two of them and their four children down the road to restoration. It was very, very difficult as you can imagine. After a few months they told us that they never were legally married and wanted to have a legal ceremony and leave the streets once and for all. They asked if we would be the witnesses for the ceremony and I said, "We can do better than that…we want to take care of the whole wedding reception." I cooked an awesome meal of filet mignon, grilled chicken, rice and beans, and our staff served all of the people. We even had a photographer friend take pictures. It was a beautiful night that ended with worship and the newlyweds sharing with friends and family all that they had walked through. They did leave the streets and are still happily married and we consider them great friends.

This story is proof that God is a God of restoration and redemption. He's not in the disposal or even recycling business—He makes all things new. The last prophecy of the Old Testament speaks of Jesus and it says, "He has come to restore the hearts of the Father's to their children and the hearts of the children to their fathers" (Malachi 4:6). A true sign of revival is the restoration of family, and this is the heart of God for our generation and every generation, that marriages would be restored, children and parents would be restored, entire families restored together. How to pursue that restoration for our generation? It begins with each couple pursuing the ecstasy of love in marriage. Perfect love casts out all fear.

As you read this book, I pray that all fear is dissolved in the radiant fiery love of the Father and that in turn you will be able to love your spouse just as the Father loves.

Nic Billman
Founder, Shores of Grace Ministries
www.shoresofgrace.com

Introduction

I married my soul mate, without a doubt. I was full of love, passion, and zeal. I was so saturated with love that forgiveness was easy. Then as years went on it seemed as though we were battling head to head, in so many issues. Things became so difficult that I had to be on my face every day before God to survive. *There has to be more! This could not be God's full intent for my life and what marriage was meant to be!*

As I continued to cry out to the Lord and seek His face, His heart, His wisdom, He called me higher. He opened my spirit to believe for greater, to believe for Him to move the mountains of impossibility. He gave me great faith to believe for the outrageous because I believed in the commitment. He started to open my eyes to what true ecstasy really was.

My whole purpose in writing this book is to share the concepts God has given me in healing, deliverance, and wisdom to align ourselves for the greatest thing we can attain in ourselves and in marriage—*ecstasy of love.* My desire is to create a greater hunger for oneness, fullness, and intimacy in every reader. My heart is to help others reach their full potential in themselves and in their marriage. It is extreme joy to me when I see others who know their purpose and who are living out their destiny. I have walked through a lot of dark places of pain for God Himself to teach me deep layers of understanding of what true Love is and how to choose Love in all things and succeed. Choosing Love is choosing Him. God is Love.

We are all on a journey, and we are a woven tapestry of each other. I do not submit to you a perfect or easy marriage. I believe understanding, giving, and receiving grace is true perfection. Quite honestly, it is easier to hold grudges and be angry than it is to forgive truly from the heart and choose Love. It is easier to be selfish than to keep digging deeper in yourself, finding more of the heart of God to give to your mate.

If you purpose to choose Love in all things, you will succeed. You will reach heights in yourself, you didn't know existed, taking you to the true ecstasy of God. If you desire awesome, radical results in your life and in your marriage, it requires awesome, radical believing and pressing for the greater.

This is a "hands-on" for those looking for a deeper, higher connection with your mate. It doesn't matter where you are…there is always more. There is always more and there is always greater because God is in the equation, so I am continuously, joyfully pressing for more! If we are apathetic about our relationship, we will get apathetic results because what we believe is critical to our outcome. *As a man thinks in his heart, so is he,* or so he will be.[1]

The things that I share are not once and done. They involve moment-to-moment daily decisions to choose Love.

We think we know what Love is. Most wedding ceremonies quote the love segments in First Corinthians 13, yet when we hit walls of frustrations and disappointments, do we then choose Love? I believe if we truly walk it out consistently, it will bind the marriage, making it increasingly stronger and helping those who are not being fulfilled in their marriages to see new perspectives and release a desire for the greater.

If I am seeking, planning, and believing to achieve fullness in my life and marriage, and if I am open to whatever that may look like, I believe I am receiving and I will continue to receive, even when I don't have proof. Part of the stability in believing, as we wait for some things while others manifest, is allowing God to carve out the details, knowing fullness is His plan and it will come.

Many people, especially women, equate Love with feelings and emotions. True Love is established higher than an emotion. Our emotions follow what we believe. If our relationship is grounded in true Love, then our emotions will adhere as we grow in it. Regardless of what we have been exposed to, Papa is always calling and drawing us higher to Him, which is true Love, to receive Love (Him), to give Love (Him), and to be as He is—Love.

Initially it may appear very elementary to share what I do about each piece of Love. You may think, *Yeah, I know this,* as you look for some greater truth. But the greater truth is the layers that are in Love. The revelation is in the true place of testing in the hard places and clinging to Love when being angry is easier, when everything else is easier.

I challenge you to test every part of your heart against this authentic Love, and not just today but every day and in every moment of conflict. I am continually finding where God is calling me higher in choosing Love, especially in conflict. If you want change and you want awesome radical results, be willing to look at and deal with yourself radically. Have the courage to take the steps to make your heart and attitude adjust to Love.

We do govern our destiny. We will measure up to what our ideologies expect, high or low.

Having a successful life and marriage is not because everything is perfect in your life or because your mate is perfect in every way and meets all your needs. Success is measured in your ability to adapt to Love. There is a fulfilling that comes in the Spirit that only God can bring as you desire to be filled with Him.

⇥◊◊◊◊⇤

My heart's desire is to give explanation and reference, to hopefully answer every angle of questioning; yet to also expose places of bondage that many of us do not want to talk about. There are things we may not want to embrace, but they cause major hindrances in our ability to attain fullness of purity. If we have a standard by which we measure and compare, it helps keep us consistent in reaching our goals.

I do not believe there is or ever will be a greater standard than the Word of God. Everyone needs to affirm this truth for themselves. The best way is to test it. Take a season of your life and ask God to make Himself real and the power of the Word to be released in your life. Test what true Love is and see if it revolutionizes your perspectives. Test and see if the joy and peace in this Love doesn't call you deeper, not to mention release you into freedom. What do you have to lose?

I have several thoughts about the Word of God: First, I believe the Word of God is living, active, and can powerfully change lives if we adhere to it. I am fully convinced that it is absolute Truth whether we believe it or not. God will not force His ways upon us so it is our choice to believe, adhere to it, and apply it to our lives. The Bible is not simply a history book. The Word became flesh. The written Word of God became flesh. Jesus is Truth whether we believe it or not.

At times I capitalize Truth and Love because they are deeper than understood concepts. I want to emphasize His person in the applied truth. Since God is everywhere, I am on a journey to find Him in every sense. With no apologies, I have tried to give the reference for my perceptions and convictions in the Word.

I believe we should listen to each other's hearts because God speaks through us, but ultimately we need a higher standard for why we believe what we believe. We are held accountable to what we believe, so taking someone's word without affirmation from the Word of God is not wisdom to me. Each one of us sees only in part right now, so I believe it is wise to always be teachable in all ways.

What we believe also needs to be greater than whatever was passed on to us by our heritage. We can pass really awesome things on to our children, but I believe it needs to be more than just that. I believe we as individuals have to choose what we believe and take ownership of that revelation. Better stated, I believe every individual needs to have his or her own walk and relationship with Christ. I try to lead, teach, train, and model a relationship with God to my children in all ways, but I feel there comes a time early on, when they have to walk their own walk with Him.

Second, I do understand there are many different perceptions of how we can apply the Word of God. Some may feel that the Old Testament is no longer valid in today's concepts, for Christ has already come, and to apply modern aspects or to receive it now as manifested would be faulty. Jesus came to fulfill the law of the prophets. I believe the Word is progressive revelation. I believe it is prophecy that has happened, that is happening, and will happen.

I believe the Word is layered with deep truths that we can only embrace so much at a time, in layers, because we need to process it, allow it to evolve and open our minds for the new revelation. The revelations of the Word that I share are what Papa has taught me. We are imperfect in ourselves, but God does provide a pathway of wisdom, revelation, and help to guide us, protect us, and keep us steady on this journey of success in life—if we heed Him.

I continually apply His revelations to my life through experience by asking important questions like: How do I know if this is real? How do I know if what I hear is some great profound revelation or a made-up doctrine? I ask the questions, then I test what I sense or feel I am hearing! God will affirm His heart and His direction, if I am willing to listen. The same is true for you.

Sometimes we ask Him a question but we aren't willing to hear the answer quite yet, or we don't prepare our hearts to hear something new and different; then, I believe, it takes a lot longer to receive that revelation. But God is so faithful in helping us move into that place to hear Him, to hear Truth. Effective testing has to be from an open, teachable, humble heart.

Affirming God's Heart

Sometimes knowledge of the Word comes before the experience of God in it. Sometimes it is the adverse; yet experiencing the manifestations of

God enraptured by the Word of God confirming all at once has to be my favorite way to embrace Him.

If I have learned anything in my journey with Papa, it's that I have so much to learn because the wisdom that God pours out is so vast! He is always doing something new and breaking me free of sheltered thinking. I believe we are in the day when Jesus said that the Holy Spirit, whom the Father would send, will teach us all things and will remind us of everything He says to us and that He leaves us His peace.[2]

When we are affirming God's heart, when we are testing and trying to adhere to Him and His ways which are higher, He leaves us His peace. Fullness of peace is in our spirits and leads into our minds, if we allow it. Sometimes we discern with our spirits first, because the theology in our heads doesn't have an awareness of that Truth yet.

Sometimes it is the opposite if we have to process through a lot of unknown fears. I say this because I am very analytical, or at least, I used to be. Everything had to make logical sense or I didn't believe. Well, we know that's not faith, don't we? True faith is the substance hoped for yet not seen. It is impossible to please God without being able to believe without seeing.[3]

There have been times when I have had to receive from God through my spirit having peace because I didn't have the knowledge of the Word in that experience yet, or I was so logically minded that I didn't have room for this new move of God—especially if it didn't make logical sense. I share my perceptions in the hope of easing conflicting questions that try to steal from the freedom Christ has given you. May Papa take you to a whole new perception of who He is!

❧⟡❦

I say all of this to come back to the core heart of who I am. I am nothing without Christ. I could not write this book if it wasn't for Him doing it in me.

If you do not know Christ as Lord of your life, I encourage you in this that if you open yourself to Him—you will not be disappointed! Many say a prayer and invite Him in, but few walk with Him daily. This is not an issue of where you are going when you die, it is an issue of living this breath of life, this fragment of time He has given you, with all that you are in Him— reaching goals and dreams you never thought possible and fulfilling your destiny!

— 1 —

Pursuing Excellence

WHAT would happen if we chose excellence in marriage? Excellence is to give 100 percent of ourselves to success. Have we already chosen excellence? I think we all assume we have, but as time continues, do we actively keep this goal, purposely?

Excellence—giving all of my heart in being everything I was created to be to my husband, whether I felt like it in the moment or not. As I chose to be Love and give Love regardless of circumstances, Love (God) began to expand in me, into all of my being. It grew in all of my emotions, even where pain and anger tried to take residence. As I continually sowed those seeds of Love, my husband started choosing the same; because, I believe, God (Love) is desirable. It covers a multitude of pain and frustrations. It causes so much peace and joy; it is contagious.

Excellence is knowing that we may stumble, we may fall, but we are free to get back up again, dust ourselves off and continue with the hope of reaching the goal. What is the goal? Excellence pursues success in not only marriage, but in every area of life, as well as individual success in our personhood, establishing a relationship with Love. Because the truth is, we can not love others if we do not love ourselves properly and succeed in fullness.

In excellence there is no shame, no condemnation. It is not perfection! Perfection sets a standard in your mind that if you don't attain it, you've failed. If perfection is a part of, or is the avenue in the motivation of how you get from where you are to where you desire to be, I can guarantee that you will not achieve the goal, and the heart of failure will be hard to disengage.

What if you knew there was a level of intimacy, an ecstasy, within yourself and within your marriage that you could not attain unless it was saturated in purity and love; real unadulterated love. Would you do everything in your being to pursue it? If you knew there was a place of ecstasy, a heightened place of intense joy and passion within yourself that God has desired for you and your marriage, would you desire it? Would you do whatever it takes to align yourself to move in it?

Many of us have heard Truth in our lives, Scriptures from the Word, yet even when we believe it is Truth, we don't act on it. We don't change and align ourselves for the fruit that is promised by it. We may not realize the places of unbelief that may be in us and are surrounding our mindsets because we are more about logic and reasoning. Everything has to make sense; and yet, if we are promised success, promised prosperity, then why don't we do everything in our being to embrace it? Does that make more sense?

Many of us think *Here and now is what's important,* or *Show me and I will believe it.* Truly some things in life, such as breaking strongholds and experiencing the freedom that comes from it, we just have to test out and experience the breakthrough to believe. What do we have to lose, anyway?

Many of us do not know Truth or we do not have a standard of it in us, so we sway in our thinking not being able to embrace the fullness for which we were initially created. I doubt we realize how much we can be moved in our thinking until we are hit with extremely hard times or places in our life or marriage. When the grapes are on the wine press, then we start to see what is really in us...or not. When we are pressured by life, it exposes what we truly believe.

It also aches my heart to see so many people who know Truth, God, the Word and can recite precept upon precept, yet don't know within themselves the power of it being in them.[4] Something is definitely amiss. Because we are all made with extreme purpose and given a radical destiny, why do we settle for less?

Do you believe it? Do you believe you were made with extreme purpose and have a radical destiny? He has given you the power to choose whether or not to walk in it. *Do you know your purpose in this life, your purpose in your marriage?*

If we want success, excellence, and fullness, we have to perceive the vision. Without a vision people perish, they will not connect with fullness![5] If we realize the vision God has for us and has had for this time in our lives and in the future, it empowers us to not settle for less. If God's vision is nothing but success, who wouldn't want it? Now this, to me, is common sense, logic and reasoning.

If you desire to embark on this journey of excellence in your marriage or set the bar higher, a few requirements are necessary:

- Be a better listener in assessing where problems lie.
- Be willing to change and evolve.
- Be willing to be loving, more than you are right.
- Be open to the vision that expands as you go. (Meaning, you don't have all of the answers, but trust they will come.)
- When everything seems to be completely whacked out in the moment, discipline yourself to press into Papa for the answer, rather than, running away or to an addiction to numb the pain.
- Be purposeful to get your resolve.
- Live in forgiveness.

So how committed are we to this marriage, to success, to becoming all we were created to be? We say we are fully committed but when things seem impossible, do we give the same answer? This is the true test, when all the chips are down. What do we choose? Love?

We were created and made for the impossible, so why are we shocked when the impossible manifests right in front of us? **Impossibilities are God's invitations to opportunities for those who believe!**[6]

The only cost is you evolving, changing, opening your perceptions, trading up pride for humility, letting go of trying to make it happen, and being willing to believe outrageously!

I will also say, some of us have had a righteous father in our lives who wasn't perfect but showed us God's love in his own way, and we have been blessed to be able to see God the heavenly Father easier in relationship because of this earthly father.

I do understand there are those who have not had the experience of knowing a righteous dad, let alone have a father who would love, protect, and always be there. Having a daddy who would always build them up and encourage them, despite their mistakes, one who always pointed out the good, would have changed their lives tremendously.

If I am describing your lack of a good father figure, I encourage you, if you have not already done so, to work on letting all of the disappointments of your earthly father go, and allow God to present Himself anew and continue to do so. I point directly to the father as reference because God relates to us through the father entity; but all leadership and authority affect our viewpoints. Ask God to heal that part of you so you can receive properly from Him.

We have a tendency to view Christ through the leadership structure we have had or have lacked.

If your parents were there physically for you growing up, but not emotionally, you may tend to think that you aren't as important to God as you really are. You may not know how much your life and opinion matters to God.

If your parents were extremely strict, good parents in general, but strict, you may have a tendency to think you have to earn approval; you may feel every time you make a mistake there is a great punishment coming.

Only God can heal our mindsets to see Him for who He really is. He longs for us to see Him in Truth and Love, as He *is* Truth and Love.

I choose to believe Love in every situation in life. I choose to believe that all parents do the best job that they know how at the time. Most parents probably parent a lot by what they were taught and tried to do better by changing what they understood was negative in their growing up. Believing Love, the best, can set you free.

We cannot give what we never had unless God supernaturally overrides that, and He can and He does, but I do not usually see Him do it uninvited. God's ways are not our ways.[7] He in and of Himself never disappoints. He is peace, kindness, goodness, joy…even when He disciplines, it is in Love. It is balanced. It is not out of control, angry, or abusive.

If this is speaking to your heart; you will benefit most in your life and marriage when you align yourself in the truth of who He really is and acquire all that you were created for, otherwise you will miss out!

Marriage: What Did I Really Sign Up For?

What did we really commit to when we said our marriage vows?

What is our true heart's desire in marriage? Do we have an active goal and desire that we continually aim for, or are we firing off in every direction assuming we will hit it?

On our wedding day we are filled with excitement, hope, and vision; then what? Do we daily do everything on our part to bring peace, joy, and love to the marriage? A completely full and satisfying marriage is a full-time, 24-7 job. It is not about having and getting everything just right. We do not want a perfect marriage, well, perfect sounds great, but it is not reality. A marriage of excellence brings fulfillment; a life where we nurture each other's hearts, learning to be sensitive to one another and asking God to fill in where we lack is reality. If we align our hearts, we will embrace the fullness. It means we can make mistakes, and we are committed to forgive each other from the heart. Where our heart is there will our treasure be also.[8] What we focus on is our treasure.

My heart's desire is extreme, intense love and passion, so it is my focus. It's a daily decision I make to meet the desires of my spouse to the best of my ability by asking God to pour into me, so I can pour the overflow into him.

It's not walking on eggshells or running after a spouse to please him or her. It's being all we were created to be: being Love to each other; choosing to make it our joy to adorn our mate with pure, unadulterated love. We cannot do this in and of ourselves. If we try to live this life on our own, we sell ourselves short of our God-intended destiny. We were created for oneness with God, then oneness with our spouse; this is how we align to embrace fullness. We have to actively desire it, pursue it, and prioritize it.

PRIORITIES

The alignment in healthy and right priorities, in what we were destined for, is:

- First, our hearts toward God.
- Second, our hearts toward our spouse.
- Third, our hearts toward our children.
- Fourth, our hearts toward work, caring for extended family, and then into serving others.)

It is discipline to keep these priorities in the right order. This is not to say we have a sick child and choose to attend to our husbands first; that isn't love.

It is an ongoing posture of the heart. If we consistently try to keep right priorities, then grace fills in the gaps. I believe keeping each priority aligned is a discipline of the heart and a walk with God, posturing ourselves to constantly receive from Him.

Focusing on how I am called to pour into my husband, and being an encourager of what he needs and longs for is vital in a healthy relationship. I am not trying to be God to him, but being all of the helpmate I was designed to be for him. If I find myself pouring into my children and sense my husband is being sold short, I simply back up, regroup, and go again.

If we get the foundations built right, then there is greater strength that comes in the midst of trials. The same is true for husbands and their call to their wives.

There is much grace to make mistakes when our hearts are aligned. This is not permission to get sloppy or apathetic in our choices, yet there is no condemning ideas that can pin us down. Unless you come in agreement with condemnation, then it's a heavy guilt and shame that changes the rate of progression. What you agree with increases in strength—negative or positive.

MY NEEDS OR YOUR DESIRES,
MY DESIRES OR YOUR NEEDS?

How many times do we hinder others because we go after our own needs being met, or we are so driven by our desires that we didn't take time to even assess another's heart in the equation, especially our mates. Well, they are always going to be there, right? They're committed till "death do us part," right? Is that really Love?

Do we take for granted the very gift in front of us? If excellence is our goal, then love is the full target. It truly is better to be loving, more than it is to be right—but in the heat of the moment, it feels better to be right.

I believe it is wise to continually ask yourself if you are operating in an argumentative and/or controlling spirit. I ask myself continually, *Do I have to have the last word? Do I always have to be right? Do I have a need to prove my point and make sure he agrees with me?* Fullness in success and life depend on your heart being teachable and flexible.

Honestly, sometimes it does give temporary comfort, even power, to get our own way; yet if we are willing to look at the bigger picture from the desired end result, it disarms negative power. We can recognize that our motives are good when we do not want to promote conflict, though we can miss the fullness when we avoid confrontation in love because we fear conflict and cling to what is easier. Denying ourselves and not dealing with our true desires and passions only negate true ecstasy, peace, and joy. Denial muffles and stifles who we are. This, I believe, leads to affairs, addictions, and other negative behaviors because our true passions are not released or stirred as they were meant to be.

The motive of our heart can be truly to help our mate, yet even in that we could be denying them fullness for themselves and hindering fullness for our destiny as a couple by doing things in the relationship they are called to do. We can want so much for them that we actually prevent them from stepping up to their rightful place in the marriage, stifling them and their success in moving forward.

PAINT THE VISION

My desire as a wife is to be madly and passionately in love with my husband even beyond eighty years of age. This is the picture I continue to paint for my husband and what it looks like to me seeking his perceptions and desires: At 80 it means still holding hands, still interested in and committed to each other. I believe it is extremely important to continually paint your desire as a picture or a vision for your spouse. It has to be full of love, full of beauty, not selfishness, but oneness and how it translates to you both. This is a way of setting awesome goals and talking out your desires, and being aware that some desires and perspectives may change. There are no guarantees of certain end results, but it does set you up for success and help to set in motion the united vision.

In Love, there is a desire for unity, though sometimes the opposing arguments are louder. Only priority and discipline will make it a reality; questioning and studying your mate's desires and wanting to fulfill them together. If you want the spark and the passion to still be obvious, it doesn't just come by happenstance. I have heard so many times that the honeymoon wears off. I don't believe it has to be like that. I have been with my husband twenty-six years, married for twenty-one years. We have had a lot of awesome times, as well a, hard, intense, God-you-have-to-do-something-or-it's-all-going-fall-apart times.

We were never promised a life without any troubles. We were promised that God would never abandon us.[9] He has given us His peace. He gave us the Holy Spirit and always a way through. This is truly far greater; to know Him and His power running through us, rather than Him making our lives perfect. Although perfect seems attractive in chaos, His ways truly are greater!

We need to have a goal of desiring fullness and oneness in our marriages continually on the forefront of our minds. Do we assume we have these goals from the start? We take our vows: till death do us part, and we agree to become one, but if it starts to get tough, divorce is always an option in the back of our minds, or we may think death meaning my love for that person died because of so much pain…then it's over. Many think it can never be restored and believe this way as a safety net, an escape route, even subconsciously, maybe not realizing their fears.

We may think we don't have fears, but to react with controlling mannerisms and a domineering attitude or walking away usually means there is an underlying fear that manipulates these choices. It takes humility to look at our heart's true motives. We can say absolutely anything, but the truth is in what we do.

Many couples don't even get married nowadays because they want to give their relationship a test run, fear failure, or to make sure they are with the right person. Some may disagree, but fullness will not come apart from purity. It cannot because they are of the same entity.

We want to give love, having our mate truly receive, and we want to be loved as our heart longs for without fears, manipulation, or control as part of the equation. Some may not have realized that we don't really believe for ourselves and/or our marriage the heights of awesomeness we can achieve. We think to believe outrageously for our relationships will only set ourselves up for failure thinking, *Well, what if it doesn't happen? No one is perfect. It is, what it is. I can't make my spouse love me in the way my heart longs for.* We need to believe outrageously if we want outrageous results. We simply need faith to believe for greater. I believe Faith is asking us, *What if it the greater does happen?* So, how do we posture our hearts for greater?

God very much wants us to be free in who we are. He is always doing a new thing in us and around us. He wants us to posture our hearts in a place of receiving and releasing Love. He wants us to learn how to adapt to the oneness that is before us. If we adapt to a way of doing things that is not healthy and we become driven in that way, we will miss the fullness of God. Having a standard based on the Word is solid. It is unmovable and unchangeable, because God Himself never changes. He is pure and true. His Word guarantees your success! If He is all about goodness and righteousness, then He sets the standard—and to press on, there is no better encourager than He.

If we set standards in and of ourselves we can become wishy-washy depending on our circumstances and emotions. If we have standards based on how we were raised to think and they are positive and solid from the Word, that's great, but if not, then we can find ourselves very frustrated.

So what do you believe? Do you believe you were designed and created for and with a purpose? I believe you were designed for this day and this hour. Posture your heart to believe. God has given you breath for awesome purposes that can only be fulfilled in Him.

Empowerment comes when we learn that full purpose.

If we believe that God has a plan for our lives, plans for good and not evil, plans to succeed, and excellence, then would we be challenged in believing for greater, for success? Believing for greater is always growing and always expanding so it does not matter where we are now, we are invited to believe for greater!

The Word of God is absolute Truth, whether we believe it or not. Truth is a person: Jesus. The Word became flesh. The Word is living and active. It is not simply a great history book. It is sharper than a double-edged sword.[4] It exposes, analyzes, and judges the very thoughts and purposes of the heart.

If He never changes, then I must change, because I certainly don't have those qualities—goodness and righteousness—in and of myself. Oh, sure, I can be loving and nice momentarily, until things get really intense and hard. I need the power, the love, and the strength of God daily. I also don't want to be playing in a muddle puddle, thinking I have the best when there is an ocean freely available to me. I don't want to miss out! I believe there is an endless ocean of goodness just for us; and I also believe we will *not* miss anything if we choose to live in Him. ***No good thing*** *will He withhold from anyone who walks upright,* who walks with Him.[10] It is a choice to align ourselves to walk in excellence which is and leads to success.

Many may be able to quote the following Words but do we really believe them as Truth in our lives? When things get intense, seemingly impossible, do we still believe for the greatness that is promised?

> *For I know the thoughts and plans I have for you says the Lord, thoughts and **plans for welfare and peace** and not for evil, to give you a hope in your final outcome* (Jeremiah 29:11 AMP).

> *...... **plans to prosper you** and not to harm you, plans to give you hope and a future* (Jeremiah 29:11 NIV).

> *...... **plans for welfare and not for calamity** to give you a future and a hope* (Jeremiah 29:11 NASB).

He is committed.

> *Commit to the Lord whatever you do, and **he will establish your plans*** (Proverbs 16:3 NIV).

> *Roll your works upon the Lord [commit and trust them wholly to Him; He will cause your thoughts to become agreeable to His will, and] so shall **your plans be established and succeed*** (Proverbs 16:3 AMP).

He teaches the right posture of our hearts that **guarantees** success!

> *Blessed (happy, fortunate, prosperous, and enviable) is the man who walks and lives not in the counsel of the ungodly [following their advice, their plans and purposes], nor stands [submissive and inactive] in the path where sinners walk, nor sits down [to relax and rest] where the scornful [and the mockers] gather. But his*

delight and desire are in the law of the Lord, and on His law (the precepts, the instructions, the teachings of God) he habitually meditates (ponders and studies) by day and by night. And he shall be like a tree firmly planted [and tended] by the streams of water, ready to bring forth its fruit in its season; its leaf also shall not fade or wither; and everything he does shall prosper [and come to maturity] (Psalm 1:1-3 AMP).

My condensed understanding of this is: You are blessed (happy, prosperous) if you seek wisdom and advice from people who are walking in purity and right choices. You will be successful in life if you do not hang out mindlessly with people who are rebellious, bitter, critical, and judgmental; rather, be very purposeful and intent concerning your choices in life. Your joy is in being in Him and knowing Him, whether in Word and/or Spirit, day and night. In this, He causes you to be so firm in who you are in Him that you become stable, making you immovable, producing goodness and fruit to share with others. In this, He promises that everything you do will prosper and come to maturity. This again is not about being perfect; it is about excellence, trying your best. Okay, condensed maybe not, but you must agree quite appealing for those who desire success.

Let's judge for ourselves the standard that He sets. It is easy to say we believe. He wants to cause us to succeed, but in the face of what looks like poverty, chaos, or extreme heartache, do we still believe fully as we wait for it to be manifested? Dare to believe!

A Legacy

Seeing the percentage of divorce rates continually increasing, I believe if we want a different result than the status quo, then we need to make different, purposed decisions, believing for greater. Even Einstein said to do the same thing over and over expecting a different result is insanity. If we want the next generations to be more empowered, then we need to be more empowered. I don't want to hand this next generation a model of marriage that stays together because that's what you do, or stays together for the kids, or a marriage on paper only. I want to leave a legacy that is more—much more!

Do we try to live every moment as though it were our last, pushing for excellence, wanting to leave an honorable legacy? Do we think that far ahead in the busyness of life? **I believe we were created for so much more than what we have seen and experienced so far, more than what we see manifesting!** I believe fullness is actively growing and releasing in the earth, but it's coming through the heart of desire; being willing, being humble enough to ask for help. Whether it's asking God for help and listening, then obeying, or in the moment listening to the godly counsel that He leads us to, we need to be alert and then heed His wisdom.

Pride, whether insecurity or conceit, will prevent you from attaining this fullness for which you were created. Pride says, *I don't need help*, I will figure it out myself." Insecurity speaks with the uncertainty of deserving or the worthiness to ask for help.

There can also be the issue of laziness or ignorance of our identity. It says, "Whatever is going to happen, will happen, this must be God's plan for my life. This must be the thorn in my life I am supposed to carry." They assume God's will is full in front of them, yet they don't ask God for help or they don't wait on Him, they don't make time for Him. Then when all chaos breaks out they assume this is God's finest for them.

In reality, we have to spend time with Truth to know It, to trust It, to lean on It. I am not talking about church on Sunday. Church on Sunday can be great if your heart is there. **We do not mature by the things we do, but by the right relationships we have with the Creator and with each other.**

There is no overnight remedy to fix things. It is a life refined. If we have submitted ourselves and the situation to the Lord, then wait on Him, trusting, then we have to know that He is fully in the midst of our hard times and extreme pain. He never abandons us, even if we feel He does; that's not Truth, that's not who He is. He is a Gentleman. He will not force Himself on us. He waits to be invited—such Love. Once we practice believing Truth, then our emotions will follow.

Pursuing fullness and excellence first has to be by desire, followed by humility and a molding into this oneness. There are no guarantees of life spans or even of our mate's choices, but there is the promise of Love always being in us and with us, a never-ending supply. Simply, God is love—and His Love is being poured out constantly. It's an ever-flowing, constant resource. There is no beginning or ending; it just is. If we are tapped into the truth of who He is and who we are in Him, we are completely equipped and aligned for Love to flow into and out of us.

The understood reality is that we cannot give what we do not have. We have to first receive God's love, then we can release it. It can only come by choice and a desire to give your mate the finest, not focused on what you will get, but being filled by God so you can pour the overflow into your spouse, knowing your needs will be fulfilled. That fulfillment can come through your spouse or can come supernaturally through your relationship with Christ, If you're aligned it is a continuous flow. The fullness is in this posture—a constant keeping ourselves aligned in Him to grow in this equipping.

The greatest thing you can desire is to truly choose to love, to give real love, unconditional, untainted love.

I am going to preface this next direction of thought with those who have heard the Word most of our lives, yet we may not be cultivated in allowing the Word to continually break up fallow ground inside us. Sometimes we become desensitized to the power that is released through the Word because we think we know it. The Word is living. The Word became flesh. So knowing it, living it, being and becoming the Word is life—not simple memorization. The Word has many, many layers and there are always more layers to be revealed. If we are not careful, pride can form a wall of, *I know this, it's not new*, then we miss the Revelation (Jesus) in the moment. Wisdom is always looking for the new even in the appearance of what perceives to be known or old. This is humility, being teachable. A broken contrite heart He will not reject.[11]

Having said all of that, I encourage you to read the following verses from the chapter of love looking for the new layer, new revelation of how it applies right now to your life. This is one of the best ways to hear God speak.

> *Love endures long and is patient and kind; love never is envious nor boils over with jealousy, is not boastful or vain/glorious, does not display itself haughtily. It is not conceited (arrogant and inflated with pride); it is not rude (unmannerly) and does not act unbecomingly. Love (God's love in us) does not insist on its own rights or its own way, for it is not self-seeking; it is not touchy or fretful or resentful; it takes no account of the evil done to it (It pays no attention to a suffered wrong). It does not rejoice at injustice and unrighteousness, but rejoices when right and truth prevail. Love bears up under anything and everything that comes, is ever ready to believe the best of every person, its hopes are fadeless under all circumstances and it endures everything [without weakening]. Love never fails [never fades out or becomes obsolete or comes to an end]…So faith, hope and love abide… love—true affection for God and man, growing out of God's love for us and in us…* (1 Corinthians 13:4-8,13 AMP).

A life that manifests these true attributes of Love doesn't appear on you all of a sudden one day, though God can and does at times manifest it instantly upon you and in you, if He so desires to reveal Himself this way. I believe His heart so delights in our desire to choose Him, to choose Love when it's easier to do anything else. It is so much easier to be selfish, which is a blatant contradiction of Love. There is so much reward in allowing Love to captivate you and become, manifest in you. It protects. It proves itself. Love defends you.

It truly causes us be limitless. We can think that people and surroundings limit us. The truth is we limit ourselves.

If Jesus said, *I can do nothing apart from the Father,* how much more am I limited in and of myself? How much more do I need help? Yet in Him I can do *all* things—limitless!

What's the Real Deal Here?

You may be thinking, *Yeah, this is great! I feel the affirmation, empowerment, and focus already.* That's great! Or maybe you're a bit on edge with all the talk about God. You want wisdom, help, and success, but you're really not interested in jumping through hoops to get there. You may be thinking, *Okay, all right already, get on with it.* That's great, because time is of the essence, and I am not talking about religion here, as in a set of laws, rules, habits, traditions, or regulations, which are bondage. There are no hoops. It's simply about relationships, which is freedom.

Some people have been so wounded by the religious system that it has tainted their hearts toward God and they can barely handle the thought of mixing God in with helping their marriage succeed. Or on the other hand, they are completely okay with God, and it's the church stuff with which they have a hard time.

Maybe you are even wondering, *Is she going to tell me now I need to go to church to succeed or make my marriage prosper?* No, I am not! No, you don't have to go to church to have a great relationship with God. Walking with Him is not a segregated decision and in all honesty, we are the church, which is a living organism not a building.

So if we gather in Him, we are in church. He tells us to not stop gathering together.[12] (*Don't stop talking, learning, sharing, teaching,* and *worshipping together.*) I believe we need to gather together for the support and accountability that His united force brings and personally, I love gathering with hearts that are on fire for Him because it causes me to mature in Him.

He knew you would need that support and accountability but, there are no limits. That can happen anytime, anywhere. His heart never has desired for you to be in bondage to church. It is a privilege. Having a healthy perspective of God's purposes is vital.

Understanding true freedom can change our intentions. It is great to have the consistency of being poured into and pouring out! Everything in life comes back to each of us individually hearing Him; what is God speaking to you?

If we have been wounded in a Christian atmosphere, sometimes it is hard to separate the relationship with Him and the relationships with His people. When we have been hurt in any kind of organized setting, where people gather in the name of Christ, I believe it is extremely important to press through for healing and not let up until it comes. His Body is part of who He is, but we all are still learning how to let the Holy Spirit, instead of our flesh, lead us.

It is understandable to have a higher standard for God's people, an expectation to see them moving in greater manifest Love than those who don't perceive to know Him, but the truth is we are all individually on a journey, at all different levels or places. We are all crossing over different bridges of understanding at different times. And we are all held accountable for our actions and decisions.

Believers should have an obvious spirit of Love, yet I know I cannot judge or criticize another's heart. I can only focus on where my heart standards are and posture myself in the Lord as I am led. Truly, there is so much I personally need to walk in and choose, in Christ, to keep me busy for a lifetime; therefore, my focus is not on others and their choices. People are free to be themselves. I am called to love, to believe the best of others, no matter what.

Sometimes our choices in life simply expose the measure of God we know, perceive, or engage in ourselves.

Rest assured that having a relationship with God is more about *being* than *doing*. Being love. As we learn how to be as He is, we naturally want to be where He is calling and share the overflow. No striving! If we carry any kind of offense, it stifles the fullness of who we are from being released and from Christ in us to manifest. We cannot make the fruits of the Spirit come—love, peace, joy, patience, kindness, gentleness, goodness, faithfulness, and self-control.[13] They are just that, fruit. If we're grafted, surrendered, we're good; the fruit comes as we choose to abide in Him.

At this point I just want to affirm to you that I believe wholeheartedly that it is not by accident that you are reading this! Are you looking for vision? Hope? Wisdom? I do not have it in and of myself, but what I have been given, I give to you. I believe God is pouring over and in you as you read this! Whatever your heart longs for (healing, forgiveness, oneness, fullness), I stand in agreement with you, that it will come; and where two agree in harmony in Him, it shall be.[14]

Sometimes the greatest thing you can do for someone,
especially your mate, is believe in them and agree with them,
for this releases power.

If what you desire is righteous, then have peace as you wait. I can say this confidently because I have asked God to touch and draw every heart He wants to move through this, so it's Divine. It has already been ordained. You are right where He wants you to be.

Seeing how fullness probably isn't going to fall out of the sky onto your lap, you have to choose day to day, moment to moment, learning who He is and learning who you are in Him, and walking it out. **This is the greatest equipping, knowing who you really are, that you can ever attain in this life. It is an endless river of power, wisdom, and love!**

If you're serious about wanting fullness and oneness in your marriage, I urge you to consider this next step in excellence which is inviting Papa and committing to success; to the measure you apply your heart, will be the measure of your success! The pivotal point in fullness is the application of your heart.

It is extremely powerful to have you and your mate walk through this together, but if that isn't an option, for whatever reason, do not hold back any part of your heart because God will move through where He is desired! This will position you to experience and walk in true ecstasy.

I strongly encourage you to take time to hear God, His perceptions of what you are addressing. At times He will show you more to get total healing in each area as you are open to receive. This takes time and patience to ask, wait, and listen, but it is well worth the effort! Journal what you feel you are hearing and test each area with the Word.

There may be a temptation to just read on and not purposely make room to receive greater revelation and understanding.

Sometimes we may assume by just reading it, that it's in motion; desire has to lead into commitment to get results.

If you have fear, anxiety, discouragement, unbelief, lack of faith or hope... these things take up space in your sphere, so after you surrender them ask God to fill you in those places. These emotions vibrate at a lower frequency than Love, causing an undo weight and heaviness you were not ever meant to carry. His burden, His yoke is easy; it's light.

Dear Papa,

Thank You that I have an awesome opportunity set before me to live a life of excellence, that I could know this greater depth of Love and faith that You have called me to, to know You and be known by You. Thank You for a life where I don't have to be perfect, but truly do everything to my best, in You, as you will fill in where I lack.

I want to be completely transparent and real in every area of my life with You and my spouse. Even if it initially costs me the exposure of secrets, I trust You will sustain me in choosing truth, choosing You. I know that anything I choose to hide only keeps me from greater heights. I have nothing to offer You but my willingness to evolve and mold into that for which I am destined.

I don't want to sell my spouse, my children, or myself short because I choose to shrink back when it's really hard. I need Your help. Thank You. I know I receive as I learn to ask. You are my Ever-present Help in times of trouble. When Jesus said, "You will do greater!" I receive it as empowerment and encouragement. I surrender and trade up my selfishness for Your ways. Teach me how to posture my heart to receive and give Love(You). I know You are committed to me. Help me to be as committed to You and my marriage! Cleanse me from all impurity. Help me to accept the Truth that You are teaching me as I go.

I cannot change anyone else but myself, so help me change myself to be Love. Help me to align my priorities and focus of life first on You, then on my mate! Help me to submit to Your leading. Open my ears to hear Your voice more clearly. Open my eyes to see You in and everywhere You are. You said the pure in heart will see You. I believe. Cause me to be pure in every facet of my life.

Thank You for the gift of life that you have given to me, for good and not evil, a life to bring prosperity. I was formed and fashioned "For such a time as this" that You would make Yourself known to me. Help me not to be sloppy and lose focus in the busyness. Help me to trust You! Thank You that there are no strings attached, but the reality of missing greatness! Align me for everything Your heart dreamed of when You formed me. Teach me who I really am in You. Thank You for always being here for me. I believe You!

− 2 −

Defining Ecstasy

Now we are going to take excellence into ecstasy. Ecstasy is a feeling of intense joy or passion. It is an overwhelming feeling of great happiness, joy, excitement, or bliss. Ecstasy is a state of being that we allow within ourselves. It's a heightened place within us. I believe it is through relationship that we experience true ecstasy. Ecstasy is first experienced in relationship with God, through Christ, then it is through our relationships—marriage. Ecstasy is experienced intellectually, spiritually, emotionally, and also in and through purity in intimacy.

If you are single, you can attain the fullness of ecstasy in your relationship in Christ. If you are married, you can experience it with or without the understanding of your spouse. Your spouse may not be at the same place of understanding what ecstasy is or even desire it, but God doesn't hold back fullness for one because of the other. It is grand to have both husband and wife perceive, desire, and experience it, but many marriage partners are not at the same place in their spiritual walks or even in their hunger for more; yet in God's love He allows those who hunger for fullness to experience fullness.

It is also very important to understand that if we are intimate in our relationship but we have *not* made the commitment to marriage we will not be able to enter into the awesomeness of ecstasy until we align ourselves in purity.

I love the fact that we can experience fullness in and with Christ singularly, as well as together in our marriages, just because of our walk with Him; just because He wants us to experience and know Him that much. So, what is this ecstasy, how do we embrace it?

ECSTASY IN THE WORD

As we understand the original form it is taught in we can better understand it: When Jesus was resurrected and revealed Himself to the disciples, they were *filled* with this overwhelming joy, this ecstasy, this rapture—this state of being.

Picture the disciples' anticipation and excitement of seeing the One they loved so much; the One whom they walked with, trusted, and in whose presence they witnessed so many miracles. After they watched Him die, now seeing with their eyes, He is resurrected.

> *So saying, He showed them His hands and His side. And when the disciples saw the Lord, they were filled with joy (delight, exultation, ecstasy, and rapture)* (John 20:20 AMP).

You can picture this overwhelming radical joy inside them as Christ was blowing their minds by appearing.

Since this Scripture speaks of rapture, as well as ecstasy, I believe it is necessary to understand both definitions for clarity.

In John 20:20 the word rapture is given from the similar root word origin defining this overwhelming joy, yet if we study the origin root words of ecstasy and rapture we will find that they are not interchangeable words. They are slightly different in scripture references. They do not have the *exact,* same meaning.

We each only know now in part, but we each have a part so we listen, discern, and grow together. Let's elaborate on the meaning of rapture; it simply means to be caught up. Whether it translates as a state of being inside ourselves, that heightened place within like ecstasy, or as a physical movement with our flesh, both are taught in and of the Word. I believe rapture is a place that first starts in us, in our heart of worship. Here are just two implications:

Paul wrote about this in Second Corinthians 12:2 (NKJV), *"Whether in the body I do not know, or whether out of the body I do not know, God knows—such a one was **caught up** to the third heaven."*

In First Thessalonians 4:17 (ASV), Paul talks about being caught up to meet the Lord in the air. *….then we that are alive, that are left, shall together with them be **caught up** in the clouds, to meet the Lord in the air: and so shall we ever be with the Lord.*

Everyone can have a somewhat different theology of understanding so it is not my heart intent to share about theology, as much as having a desire for us, as the Body of Christ to pay more attention to the spirits that motivate us.

If we understand that ecstasy is a heightened place in us of overwhelming joy and rapture is being caught up within our spirit, with the ability to move from one geographical location to another; it is easier to see their slight differences in definition.

I believe the true focus of rapture is God's heart in being a Daddy who formed you and made everything for you, just so He could have relationship with you. He is a Daddy who sacrificed everything to give you everything, so you could learn what it is to have Him so overflowing in you and have your being so caught up in Him, in worship, in your true identity that you are raptured in Him. This can mean being translated from dimension to dimension spiritually *(in your being),* and it can mean to disappear and reappear, as was known of Elijah and Philip.[15]

Some may perceive this impossible. I will tell you this is experienced throughout the Old Testament and the New Testament. Jesus Himself models this type of rapture.[16] If you find questions rising within, I encourage you to seek the Truth for yourself. I believe every part of the Word of God—the answers are all there. Dig deeper into the meanings of the Words that are translated.

I believe that to be truly raptured is to be so full of Him, so full of His love that in our being, we are caught up, overwhelmed with joy, passion, and ecstasy and that we may move physically in spheres. Caught up in worship! I would love to see a movie about that!

As we move and press into finding this ecstasy, this overwhelming joy, contemplate and be aware of the adversities that try to come against it. It is wisdom to pay attention and evolve in our understanding of what motivates ecstasy in us.

What Motivates You?

There is a lot of theory out there that talks about rapture of the Body of Christ, but most of what I hear seems to *not* be motivated through overwhelming Joy or Love. What I hear seems to be motivated by fear—fear of missing God, fear of having to stay in a battle, and wanting God to take us out of here. I test these theories by the fruit or residue they leave. It is true, the Word does speak, *seek the Lord while He may be found*, yet we are not to be motivated by fear, only Wisdom.

God wants us to see Him as He truly is and desire to be with Him because He is fulfilling in Himself. He wants us to find Him for ourselves, out of our desire to know Him.

I have been motivated to seek God out of fear initially, these same fears of missing God. I don't believe it has been through any purposed fault of humankind, but of a spirit trying to keep the Body of Christ in bondage, keeping them from their true identity and freedom.

For some it has to be a stepping stone out of religion and into a greater relationship. God's spirit inside us continues to draw us and speak Truth causing us to desire more of who He is—Love and Peace. I believe as we allow revelation to grow inside us, we won't be content with fragments of who He is, and the hunger to know Him intimately will take over.

I want to seek God with all my heart, not because I fear what will happen if I don't. I want to walk with Him because He created me and has planned a whole life of awesomeness just for me—if I want it, just as He has for you, too. This is not a life that's perfect, but a life that through my weakness His strength is made perfect and I see Him move supernaturally and miraculously. I want to walk with Him, and in Him, because He has awakened me to His Love. Just as I want to obey man's laws, not because I have to or I will get a fine or go to jail, but because I want to, because I want to please God and I understand the purpose and His heart about them; a heart that protects.

What seems more appealing? Miracles, signs, and wonders everywhere you go or everything perfect? Yes, I understand to be with the Lord in all His fullness is our heart as the Bride of Christ, but we cannot underestimate our purpose, our timing of being here on the earth right now.

Ecstasy in Intimacy

Back to ecstasy in John 20:20: I believe this is God's desire in oneness and fullness to attain these places of ecstasy in our marriage. This is not a place of hype or one that can be conjured. Ecstasy happens when we posture our hearts right in purity ourselves, then coming together as husband and wife, inviting God into every area of our marriage, even into the deepest place of intimacy. Yes, I did just say that, intimacy. This is not attained by each partner having a perfect walk with God. It's about being open and having right relationships.

Again, we are not about perfection, but excellence. If one in the marriage opens up for ecstasy and leads, God will meet you and pour out in you. I am repeating myself on purpose because it is very difficult for those of us who want it all, but our spouse does not seem to be on the same page or for those of us who struggle with perfection being a standard. Be encouraged!

God is the One who created intimacy. He created it to bring a greater form of unity in the natural. The term "making love" is very fitting, though the act in and of itself cannot produce true and full ecstasy. It comes back to real love being the foundation. The problem today is that intimacy—sex— has had so many negative things attached to it; or if you have been abused in any way, the act can be tainted. God created it and designed it to be pure, beautiful, and a place of honoring and respecting one another. Sometimes the display of intimacy has been viewed and labeled "dirty," which shuts down places of creativity and freedom in it.

There is so much dishonor and disrespect toward the entity of men and women that has defiled our eyes, our ears, and our hearts. Abuse has made provision for hatred towards the core of who men and women are which causes affairs, destruction of relationships, and even homosexuality. The abuse that is in homes, marriages, families, and in life whether physical, emotional, sexual, and even spiritual has distorted and stolen the pure, raw form that God desired intimacy to be.

Many times when I have counseled people who have been abused they also have a core hatred towards men or women that they then need healed of. They do not always recognize it is there till we get deeper in the healing.

God can heal every area and I believe He desires to do so; but I think that sometimes we lack understanding of how much healing we may need and that we must keep pressing until we attain it. This is why, again, it is so important to have a standard to keep looking to, so we can reach these heights in excellence.

We need to have a pure view of our self, and of our mate, to attain this beautiful, unadulterated love.

I am believing with you, for you and your marriage, to not only taste ecstasy, but for you and your spouse to experience fullness, oneness, true ecstasy in your lives and in your marriage, continually!

If we ask for what Papa desires, it's a given—the answer is yes! If we just agree with one another, in the heart of God for our lives, we *will* overcome! Sometimes we just get befuddled. We get all crazy confused. Is this God's will or is this…?

There is no confusion or question whether God wants us to experience and live ecstasy—He does. I believe we need to know the heart of God for us with growing confidence. His heart is for good for us, *all* the time. Usually the distinguishing factors are timing and our hearts. Sometimes we are asking for a teaspoon, but if we would simply wait and trust, He will pour out a tractor trailer-size load.

I believe He wants to give us our heart's righteous desires! But we also need to understand that God is not going to fight with us either. If we refuse to let go of snares, He will just let us have them. He has already paved the way through and accomplished everything. The true desires of our heart are the interchange.

It's not *if* He will open up ecstasy for you, it is *when* and *how* He will open it up for you or should I say it is open from His end, you just need to connect yourself with it! He just wants you to agree with Him that He is moving inside you, in your desires. Sometimes I believe God waits for you to ask, then into maturity He draws you to press it through in prayer (spending time talking and listening to Him about it, being still in Him) and intercession—praying every angle for the fullness to be manifested, when you have no proof of the outcome, but only the unction in your spirit.

Practice Believing

There may be some gray areas in your life that challenge believing and are individually answered as in taking a certain job, buying a certain house, moving, starting a grand endeavor, and or jumping off a precipice in your life into a vision you feel God gave you. These require a lot faith to move in, and when you have a spouse, being in unity before you step into any of these areas is critical.

If you spend time talking to God, listening, and surrendering these gray areas in your life, in the midst of your time with Him, ask Him to take that desire away if it's not in Him. Then follow what He shows you, not what He can give you through it. If after seeking Him, the desire is still there or the decisions become clear, trust that answer and desire in you! *Delight in the Lord and He will give you the desires of your heart.*[17] **Delighting is the emphasis as it is the prerequisite to the fulfillment.** Then, believe what you sense and hear! As you progress in your relationship with God, you start to lift your head higher to focus on Him, to see as He sees.

So, what if it does take ten years to see your vision manifested? The greatest part is the journey with Him, preparing you along the way; He is your peace and joy. In the midst, there comes a knowing that He is moving those things, and *He* becomes the focus, instead of the vision or the desire. As people think in their hearts, so they are. It is critical for us to be sensitive to what motivates us, love or fear, because the power that He gives us in our thinking is incredible.

We are entrusted to think righteously, not positive, because of a new age perception, positive is God's perception. The glass is always half full from His angle because He is hope.

Well, you know what? As I say that, I perceive God is so full of believing that He probably looks at that half-filled glass and rejoices at the fullness that is in it) and then it manifests and becomes full! I believe this is where He is taking us as His Bride in believing and seeing. I love God's perspective. He sees everything from the finished end. He said on the cross, "It is finished!" It is done.

If we can just remind ourselves of what Papa's perspectives are compared to our perception in the midst of chaos, it will change the whole moment. It could change everything in the depths of a heated disagreement with our spouse.

Disagreement is the word we used when we matured out of fighting. Honestly, I think it is healthy to disagree so we can sharpen one another and find greater truths! It is good to express our desires, listen for wisdom, and mold to oneness as we exercise being Love to one another. **Unity does not mean we think exactly the same way.** I believe unity means deferring to one another, submitting to one another, allowing each one to think differently, but coming together for a unified purpose and agreement—relationship. As we work Love in our hearts, greater unity comes.

The next time you may be hurt or annoyed, *picture* your spouse from the end resolve, healed; honoring you, understanding you, and both of you being able to embrace your differences. Work toward living lives that are quick in forgiveness, knowing *(believing)* you both are growing greatly in loving one another. This is the vision Love creates as the goal.

Perception is everything. Speaking out what Love is saying, the opposite of what is happening, to decree it so it shall be established.[18]

If you are feeling alone in your marriage, practice believing and speaking, *I am not alone.*

The Truth is, Christ is always in us and with us, so it is impossible to be alone. It is a lie to believe we are alone. Yes, we have desires in our flesh and needs even; but as we change our perspective, we ask God to fill those desires, and He will—whether supernaturally we experience Him embracing us in the spirit to the flesh, or He may move through our spouses. The focus is Him fulfilling our needs. If we're feeling alone, our emotions are responding to what we perceive and believe—we need to choose to change our perspective.

If we change our perceptions we will change our lives, just by coming into agreement with what God is already doing. We cannot change or control people, but as we remove the negative thoughts, the atmosphere changes, and then the Holy Spirit is free to move over us and our spouses to help us see and experience truth, posturing us for ecstasy. This alone creates an atmosphere of anticipation of God's goodness and awesomeness; we cannot help but to be stirred to embrace it.

> *Father God, would You open the heavens over us, over our mates, and our family? Would You break our hearts for what breaks Yours? Would You teach us what true ecstasy is and how we compromise it by our beliefs? We want to have You in every area of our lives and marriage the way You desired from the beginning. Make us sensitive to Your Spirit and help us to walk in step with You. Train us in Your purity. Would You cause Your Love to abound greater in us, through knowledge and depth of insight that we would discern what is valid, prize what is excellent, and be untainted? We ask believing; and because this is Your desire, it is already moving and*

manifesting in us. Thank You that we ask for help, and help out of the heavens always comes to us!

Thank You for finishing in me what You have started. Thank You for opening my eyes to true Love, so I can be Love as I choose to walk in You, in this life! Thank You for the joy that infiltrates my heart, my marriage, and my home because of inviting You into it at a greater level. Remind me to continually invite You. I long to know You as Daddy!

— 3 —

Fighting for Your Destiny!

IF we desire ecstasy in our marriages, we need to assess what may hinder and be fighting against its fullness! When we start to understand the power of a unified front, as husband and wife were meant to be, we become more active in exposing the encumbrance of the enemy's lies, not allowing him to steal anymore!

Sometimes we are quick to believe in the existence of God in many multi facets, and yet we may not take the time to consider the thoughts of adversity that are working against us, understanding the Word in these areas. We must purposefully learn how to stand strong, be victorious, and contend in our spirits for the greatness that is promised to us.

The enemy does roam around like a lion looking for those he can steal from and destroy what they were purposed for.[19]

What if in every place of conflict we purpose to remind ourselves of this Word? If we remind ourselves, it must not be out of fear, but wisdom, which is the opposite of fear. If we remind ourselves out of desire and purpose to not relinquish any ground with which we have been entrusted, this kind of Wisdom will keep us focused on the course, causing us to be proactive in guarding our peace.

If we can see the bigger picture, I believe we will be more purposed about being responsible with each other's hearts.

Jesus told Peter that satan wanted to sift him as wheat (as he does us).[20] Jesus responds with saying He prayed for Peter's faith to not fail him(He asked God to help him believe).

No fear! God desires us to fear nothing! His heart is for us to know and live in the fear of the Lord; which is not remotely the same. Fear of the Lord is the (very) beginning of wisdom. It is respect and honor of who God is. All other fears are just lies that we believe and give power to just because we come in agreement with them. It is not Truth, as in having fear of not being loved. It is a lie from the beginning because we *are* loved with an everlasting love.

You may have a desire to be physically loved and touched a certain way, but as you give that desire to God, He will give you your heart's desire in His righteousness. He will fulfill you, whether through your mate, or supernaturally, if your heart is focused on Him!

In pointing out what and who the opposition really is, we need to continually remind ourselves in the midst of hardships that people are not our enemies.

Your spouse is not your enemy. Your mate is half of you because you became one. It is unproductive to allow hate and other spirits to live or linger at any depth even if you feel you have grounds. Allowing the opposite of the goal you desire forfeits your moving and advancing in fullness. If you believe when you pray and pray what is True, you are free to be Love, and God will deal in each place with and for you.

If we are Love, a reflection of Him which is joy, peace, patience, kindness, goodness, self control, then the enemy is easier to expose along with his efforts to devour. Yet, if we come into agreement with the enemy's plans and purposes through fear and disbelief of God's promises, the enemy can enforce and advance his manipulations.

Our opposition is within the spirit realm. We do not fight flesh and blood.

> *For we are not wrestling with flesh and blood [contending only with physical opponents]...but against the powers [the master*

spirits]...against the spirit forces of wickedness in the heavenly (supernatural) sphere (Ephesians 6:12 AMP).

If we exercise the Truth and submit to the spirit inside us, we can dismantle the friction with others. It takes two to tangle as well as two to argue. Sometimes "praying, giving it to Papa, more than we're saying," is wisdom. Taking the authority Christ has given us against the opposition in our midst—commanding strife, fear, frustration, control, *whatever you are sensing*, to leave—subdues its ability to manipulate, as long as we're willing to just be Love.

What is the opposing lion that contradicts true ecstasy in your life?

Whether we agree or not, it is wisdom to understand what comes against us so we won't be deceived and lose what is rightfully ours.

If you are awakening to the purpose of your life, you're a real threat to the enemy. He is all about destroying the family unit—in any and every way. And it is true that when you feel like all the walls are crashing in, it is because something radical is getting ready to transpire in your life. But have no fear—God is greater and He defends those who walk with Him!

Quite honestly, a lot of those radical places may be changes in us, our becoming Love and stepping into true freedom. We need to live actively aware and know where we are headed and not be apathetic or lethargic. Live life with no regrets. Sure there are things we see in hindsight that we would have chosen differently; but now, we must live actively, moving forward purposely, without condemnation or shame, to have no regrets, making the better choices in front of us. Being aware automatically positions us. Denial is the door to destruction. We are only fooling ourselves to allow it. Just because we may not want to accept Truth does not change the absolute that it is. There is no deception in Truth!

PORNOGRAPHY, PERVERSITY, AND SEXUAL IMMORALITY

The denial and the deceptions that are entangled in pornography, perversity, and sexual immorality are some of the biggest raging lions that have come to seek, kill, and destroy. God has entrusted us with our lives. He has awesome plans, but He will not force us to walk in them. It is always a choice. One of the greatest heartaches is the fruit of people's choices that go against their destiny.

The pornography industry—yes, it is an industry—has goals to advance in generating revenue by extending its outreach. The people in control understand that the younger the person, the more likely the desire and hunger for more will be established. I believe this is why we see seductive cartoons and advertisements aimed at young children.

If you take the time to study it at any depth, you will learn that pornography is as addicting as crystal-methamphetamine, which is one of the most dangerous drugs. Crystal-meth is the easiest drug to get addicted to and one of the hardest from which to recover.

When pornography is viewed, a chemical inside the brain is released that is equivalent to the effect of drug addiction. Over time, the "pleasure chemicals" in the brain, such as dopamine, become over-used and as feedback the brain releases less of this chemical and the brain becomes starved for this release. This is why there is always desire for more; the addiction. Pornography always leaves people empty as an end result, and also at a place where they are starving for more. Pornography is a counterfeit to sidetrack us from the true ecstasy that only comes through oneness in God.

In pure and true intimacy—oneness of you, your mate, and God—is a cord of three that cannot be easily broken.[21] So understand this, if you have opened up to these oppositions whether you desired to initially or not, there is something far greater and better awaiting you. It is better than what you can imagine, hope, or dream. Also, if you have allowed pornography at any level, there is more attached to your relationship that will prevent you from stepping into the awesomeness of ecstasy. These spiritual bonds have to be diminished if you desire to experience ecstasy.

Pornography may seem simple and harmless to some, yet it can take extreme possession of us and sink its teeth deep into us. A lot of times we don't realize the stronghold until we try to lay it completely down and not return; then, the fight to be content and not engage another addiction in its place begins.

If you are already enraptured by pornography, I believe it will take extreme diligence, perseverance, and the supernatural deliverance of God to walk in freedom from it, but it is there for you if you desire. Think about it! Why would it be so easy to walk away from these strongholds when what awaits you is the authentic, pure ecstasy, something far greater and something so extravagant, that the enemy has worked extremely hard to distract and attach you to something else? Counterfeits may look like the real thing, but they do not hold the value, or the depth, and there is always a let-down at some point.

We need to be alert to the fact that there is a counterfeit to everything in the earth, right now. Satan cannot create, but he does mimic. Things can look like God, smell like God, and not be Him. For those who are disgusted by pornography, it is a no-brainer that it is not Him, but there are other areas where you may be stifled. For those who have grown up around pornography, whether you wanted it or not, the line of purity is blurred. We may think, *What's the big deal? I'm not hurting anyone. If it feels so good, how can it be wrong? It doesn't bother my spouse.*

This thinking is the deception that fools many. I promise you, in experiencing it myself, there is nothing greater than experiencing these heights of ecstasy the way God has intended, in their purest form. God has opened my eyes to walk with Him in this; He has taught me all of these Truths. I don't just have an opinion, I understand and see. I have seen the great gift God has given my husband and me in this purity. Nothing can compare!

Some may think a little bit of pornography is harmless—there is no such thing. Some would say, *It helps stimulate me and my spouse.* If you have to be stimulated by something else I believe you are missing out in the hidden-ness of ecstasy that is accessible to you and your mate. Viewing pornography sets a standard, whether it sets it for you, your mate, or what it should be together.

I feel that God wants us in our marriages to be completely stimulated just by each other, with no props.

You can only know the truth of what I am saying, if you pursue it wholeheartedly.

I do understand what it is to have props in intimacy, yet I have chosen to follow God in His desire for us to know a deeper intimacy.

There is so much more available to us than what we can ever dream. We can not know this as truth until we begin to experience the deeper places of intimacy. The idea of trying to get true fulfillment apart from purity is an oxymoron. I don't believe for a moment that God desires us to fulfill ourselves sexually, which leads me to address masturbation.

The Truth about Masturbation

Some may be appalled to read any idea on this subject, but I believe we need to embrace the reality that many people, including Christians, struggle with masturbation as well as pornography, whether we want to hear it or not. My heart again, is that I don't believe God desires us to satisfy ourselves. Many may disagree, but I feel it is an unhealthy addiction and a major stumbling block for us in becoming one in our marriage.

You will never know what has been tucked away just for you in your spouse, in intimacy, if you are distracted by counterfeits. If you are ensnared by these strongholds, Christ can set you free. Sometimes He supernaturally, all at once, delivers you, and sometimes it's through a process; it will come in whatever way is best for you to stand in that freedom. But it will come, if you set your heart to get free and focus on Him meeting your needs instead of yourself or things. **Believe until it comes, however long it takes—be relentless!**

I hope to invoke in you a passion to find these new, hidden, romantic, exotic places in your mate without anything else—just you, your spouse, and Christ. It only gets better and better if you continue to press into this purity!

I attest to excellence, trying my best in Christ, inviting Him and allowing Him to fill all of the gaps. This perseverance takes you to ecstasy. I hope you can hear my heart. I am not speaking of a perfect marriage; perfection has a standard I will never attain. I just walk on the path toward excellence that I have been led to by Christ. This thought alone causes me to exhale and enjoy the journey.

Ecstasy in God, *satisfies* with a righteous desire to evolve and grow in more.

As we are aligning ourselves to experience ecstasy the truth of what we already believe about our mate, marriage, and life is exposed when things get really difficult, when we can't have what we want and think we deserve, in the moment. When we get pressed, we see what is truly inside us. As our beliefs unfold in are places of hardship it is important to apply the Truth of what God says to overcome.

In our hearts and minds, we have to accept what Truth is in purity before we can make a stand for it.

So now that we have hit the core truths about pornography and masturbation, I don't believe we can tie it all together in understanding without talking about lust.

Defining Lust

Jesus said, "*Whoever looks at a woman to lust for her has **already** committed adultery with her in his heart*" (Matthew 5:28 NKJV).

What is lust? Lust means "Gotta have it!" We can lust after anything or anyone. Jesus wasn't saying by simply looking at a woman we lust. He was distinctly saying to look with lust as in desiring or wanting was crossing the line into adultery. This is valid either way, if even a woman would look at a man with lust, as well, or even in homosexuality.

The moment we allow it, it has already broken the vows. This is not an excuse to get a divorce upon hearing this. God can redeem and restore absolutely anything, actually that is what He majors in; redemption. However, if we took this Word seriously, would we make more cautious decisions when we are pumping gas and the attraction that could stir us appears? Would we guard ourselves more with the television, the Internet, and magazines?

Some would say, *I just want to look. There is nothing wrong with looking. Everyone looks at each other.* If I were to test the motive of my heart I would have to ask myself, *Am I okay with my husband looking in the same way?* Another question may be, *Do I get something from it? Does it give me something? Happiness, even for a moment?* Exposing these strongholds of deception that may be so interwoven in our being takes greater diligence to find Truth.

I have come through a lot of unhealthy desire for people's approval and deep insecurities because I didn't know who I was or what my purpose was to be. I know what it is like to look in all the wrong places for love and approval. I am not proud of that, but thankful for the wisdom and healing that I have attained in the process. It has given me compassion for others in the same place, and a hope for them.

It takes the desire for the pure and a mature heart to receive Truth. What we may see on television or in common magazines may be what they call "soft porn," but it still is what it is. Two do become one. Spiritual bonds can be formed when we desire and want it—even if we just want to stare at it for a moment. Sin is conceived in the mind. Lust can be very deceptive and can lead to infatuation, addiction, and adultery.

ADULTERY—ANOTHER COUNTERFEIT!

Define adultery? Most people, I believe, would answer "having an affair." I think it is broader in perspective than that. It is any act of fornication. Adultery is unfaithfulness. Being emotionally, physically, and spiritually involved with another outside marriage is adultery. Lust may or may not open the door to adultery.

It is wise to be aware of what spirit we are walking with to stay in purity. We can have emotional affairs simply in applying ourselves, not even as much with words, but with flirtation. It is spoken through our body language and sometimes our dress. Even eye contact, alone, can say a lot of words

Some may feel that I am speaking over the top, ridiculous. I have learned and continue to learn and try to be aware of what I am inviting into my sphere, because I am becoming more aware of what wants to ensnare us, as a people.

What is God's heart about adultery? I believe it is necessary to view several points in the Word to help draw the full heart of God in this. If He spoke it as one of the Ten Commandments,[22] which are foundational as "Thou shall not," I would say it is a standard of His heart. Just as well as, "Thou shall not covet your neighbor's wife," which is lust.

This spirit of adultery is not wisdom, and it's destructive.

> *A man who commits adultery has no sense; whoever does so destroys himself* (Proverbs 6:32).

> *But I tell you that anyone who divorces his wife, except for sexual immorality, makes her the victim of adultery, and anyone who marries a divorced woman commits adultery* (Matthew 5:32).

God is after purity and commitment. There is a spirit of adultery released when a man or a woman engages in intimacy that opposes the Lord.

We cannot attain true ecstasy if we have engaged a spirit of adultery, unless we take responsibility, asking for forgiveness, and ask God to break this spirit off and purify our hearts from it. This is not just repenting, turning away from it, but allowing our hearts to be broken over the interaction with it, then following through with breaking the spirit of adultery and the spiritual ties, through Christ.

(Note: I walk through accepting responsibility and getting free of these strongholds and soul ties at the end of this chapter. If the Lord is bringing things to mind, I strongly encourage you to allow your heart to view those thoughts alongside Papa's heart and allow the emotions of grieving His heart to rise in you. If you have diminished feelings causing you to feel uncomfortable toward these relationships, it is wise to allow them to surface so you can get free and experience true peace. Shunning memories will not bring true, lasting peace.)

As we weigh the Scriptures, finding awareness of Truth, I believe it is extremely important not to lose God's heart about the actions. God is just and He is merciful. His ways are not our ways, they are higher. He desires us to be pure and committed in all ways, like He is.

Jesus reminds us of God's intent for marriage and why He permitted divorce:

> Jesus replied, "Moses permitted divorce only as a concession to your hard hearts, but it was not what God had originally intended. And I tell you this, whoever divorces his wife and marries someone else commits adultery—unless his wife has been unfaithful." (Matthew 19:8-9 NLT).

If there was unfaithfulness, the mate was free to marry again, not spoken of as an adulterous, otherwise *(see Matthew 5:32)* it speaks of that spouse as a victim of adultery. If we want to walk in purity, we need to see things as they really are. I believe we need to see God's perspective of actions to see the full perimeter of what commitment really means in His Love. We want to break off everything that entangles us. Because His ways are not our ways, we need to perceive His heart. We cannot take responsibility for what we do not understand. If we are after the abundant life Jesus came to give us, taking responsibility for our actions is how we enter into it and walk it out![23]

If we understand what God thinks about marriage, divorce, separation, even violence in marriage, we then can make wise choices and purposely attain fullness and succeed!

Malachi speaks God's heart about divorce, separation, and violence:

For the Lord, the God of Israel says: I hate divorce and marital separation and him who covers his garment [his wife] with violence. Therefore keep a watch upon your spirit [that it may be controlled by My Spirit], that you deal not treacherously and faithlessly [with your marriage mate] (Malachi 2:16 AMP).

I think it is necessary to emphasize that God hates unrighteous actions, but loves people. He doesn't condemn us, but convicts to bring us to healing. He gives us directions so we can and will prosper, if we choose! Wisdom is being aware of His heart and how we allow intimacy.

Is Intimacy a Covenant?

How did Jesus view the woman at the well?

"Go and get your husband," Jesus told her. "I don't have a husband," the woman replied. Jesus said, "You're right! You don't have a husband—for you have had five husbands, and you aren't even married to the man you're living with now. You certainly spoke the truth!" (John 4:16-18 NLT).

The woman wasn't legally married, bound by paper and a ceremony, but in God's eyes she was. We need to take this seriously if we want fullness. She was spiritually tied to all of these men because of their shared acts of physical unity. I believe there is a more serious accountability we need to embrace to enable us to step into the abundant life that awaits!

And finally, what was Jesus' response to the woman who was caught in adultery, who was brought to Him to be stoned? Jesus said:

"He who is without sin among you, let him throw a stone at her first."…Then those who heard it, being convicted by their conscience, went out one by one, beginning with the oldest even to the last. And Jesus was left alone, and the woman standing in the midst. When Jesus had raised Himself up and saw no one but the woman, He said to her, "Woman, where are those accusers of yours? Has no one condemned you?" She said, "No one, Lord."

And Jesus said to her, "Neither do I condemn you; go and sin no more" (John 8:7-11 NKJV).

My translation of Jesus' response:

- Acknowledge and see it for what it is, adultery.
- Surrender it to Him, being set free.
- Go and sin no more; walk away and choose purity.

Have you ever met people who, in relationship, are involved in so-called "love-hate" relationships? They know they are not meant for each other, but they just can't walk away. The relationship eventually progresses into an extremely unhealthy situation because they were bonded physically *and* spiritually to each other and didn't realize that to be totally set free, the spiritual ties have to be broken. They are very real and have a tight hold on us!

If you have been part of any of these scenarios, there is no condemnation in Christ, but these strongholds will invoke stumbling and keep you from your destiny and ecstasy!

The awesomeness about God is His grace! He brings awareness to us so we can be empowered as we let go of what ensnares us so we can walk in Truth.

REDEFINE PURITY

In all seriousness, as we look over our whole lives so far, if we would see them as Papa does, whether we wanted to be part of certain relationships or not, could we call our lives pure?

If not, are you willing to accept the truth? Are you willing to ask God to bring it all back to memory so you can renounce it and establish true purity?

We cannot establish purity if we are not willing to take responsibility and acknowledge every action where we have either let go of it or where it was taken from us. This is not to embrace any condemning and shameful ideas, but to allow the conviction of embracing the counterfeits and redefine purity. It is purposing to take the time to see what has tainted true purity, to acknowledge what has made room in our lives and is still attached.

Unless you consciously have broken the unhealthy ties to other individuals, they are still there whether you believe it or not. The only way to test and expose darkness that may be hidden is to be willing to bring it all to the light and see it for what it is. What's the worst thing that could happen? You just might be set free! If you ask God for bread, He will not give you a stone.[24]

I believe we have barely scratched the surface of knowing what true freedom really is!

Just because we may not want something or someone anymore does not mean there are not spiritual ties to them. Every time we opened ourselves up to looking with lust or having an emotional fling or any sexual encounter, it created a tie that needs broken—and only Christ can do that for us. Sometimes freedom just simply means becoming aware, taking responsibility, and asking God to break the bonds, and then we can begin walking in wisdom and not allow that door to be opened again.

I have seen, many times, freedom come for those who confess heavy petting with another. Heavy petting may seem minute to some, but apparently not to God. Spiritual bondage can affect any part of our heart, or ourselves, that we give to another who is not our spouse. It all crosses over the line of purity.

You may not agree, but I encourage you to test what I am saying wholeheartedly. What do you have to lose but negative influences and baggage of the past?

We were never intended to live away from complete oneness. This is why there is so much pain in many hearts today. We have relinquished this gift of purity.

It is the pure in heart who will see God.[25] We are promised that we are blessed and spiritually prosperous if we hunger and thirst for righteousness (uprightness and right standing with God), for we shall be *completely satisfied*![26]

I don't believe we can easily see in ourselves where we are or have been tainted, especially when purity has been taken from us through another's control or obsession. This can happen in marriages where there is a using of one another to satisfy ourselves, instead of honor and respect. We cannot easily see what is impure when we have grown up around it all our lives, if it is socially acceptable in our heritage, or in the relationships surrounding us.

If God's love is ever-increasing and invited to manifest in our lives, it is then when we learn to discern what is pure, approve what is excellent, become untainted, and we will not stumble, nor cause others to stumble. We will then be filled with the fruits of righteousness. His glory will then be both manifested and recognized—which is pure.[27]

If we have accepted Christ as Lord of our lives, and we have invited the Holy Spirit to dwell in us, then the secret to be revealed is Christ in us, the hope of glory.[28] His Love needs to abound, ever-increasing of the knowledge of who He is in every part of our being. It is then we learn to know purity.

To pursue purity, we first invite Him in every way to abound in us. We need to be humble enough to ask God to show us impurity that we have allowed into our lives. It is maturity to listen and then be obedient to walk through the process to purify and renounce the strongholds we embrace or have been part of. We are free then to receive the cleansing and continually guard our hearts, thereafter.

> For all that is in the world—the lust of the flesh [craving for sensual gratification] and the lust of the eyes [greedy longings of the mind] and the pride of life [assurance in one's own resources or in the stability of earthly things]—these do not come from the Father but are from the world [itself] (1 John 2:16 AMP).

Understanding where things originate and assessing the outcome of their presence is wisdom. I don't want things in my life that do not bring complete fulfillment. I don't want to settle for second best at any level. Again, I have not arrived, but I want to keep advancing.

We are coming back again to personal desires and what we believe the point of this life really is. A great way to test things is if we can truly see Jesus doing it or desiring it; or if we can try to picture our children walking in it and feeling good about it. If the thought of them walking in it makes us feel unsettled, then something needs to change.

Everyone knows that our children don't do as we *say*—they do as they have *seen,* because what they see creates a standard in their minds. This remains their standard unless they experience such trauma that, with God's help, they receive strength to go in another direction.

Sometimes we can be numb to situations or the depth for ourselves, but to picture our children walking in it makes us cringe and see it for what it is. This helps expose anything we may not see in full truth at times. Whatever we allow, we hand down to our children, even in secrecy. It may even change form, but I think we need to take this responsibility for the reality that it is.

When it comes to purity there is no place for compromise that will produce good fruit in and of itself.

God can and does move through all things for our good in the end result, but that does not hold back the pain, deception, and confusion we open others up to by our decisions. It does not relieve us of consequences either.

We were created for oneness and that is why everything we do affects others as well. We are deceived to think any less. For every action, there is a reaction. We set things in motion, whether positive or negative.

There is no condemnation in Christ, just conviction. Condemnation says you're worthless, you're dirty, you should be ashamed, burdened with guilt—but conviction sees the reality of your situation and compares it to Christ and allows you to feel how you have affected His heart. Conviction pulls you to Him, then you see hope in the changes. Think about it: because

He created you for greatness and you are settling for a counterfeit, how would that grieve His heart?

It's like the rich Daddy who wants to give His daughter and son the whole kingdom, yet they are trying to establish their own. He has done an awesome work to give them everything, and yet they choose other things.

His heart isn't broken because you don't want the kingdom.
His heart aches because He knows you are missing out on
the fullness He wants to give you and He knows
you can never attain it without Him.

Trying to fulfill our carnal (fleshly) desires with anything other than through Christ hinders the full and complete vision—our destiny of excellence and purity. We need to take time to look at our hearts and our motives and ask why we allow impurity or why we are addicted to things that only temporarily satisfy. What void are we trying to fill? Recognizing God wants to not just fill the void, but overflow in and over us, if we are willing, allows us to embrace true satisfaction. There isn't anything that we could surrender and then regret, because He always pours an overflow of Himself in those areas, if we invite Him. We may have to press hard through addictions, but the outcome is so outrageously awesome that we won't regret it!

Break Away into Freedom!

At this point, if you are willing to start the process of becoming free from the strongholds and taste and experience true satisfaction, I encourage you to get a piece of paper or write in the margin of this book. Take a few minutes and ask God to show you the impurity you have been part of, or are still involved in. Write down every person's name who comes to mind; even if you hesitate, don't second guess any connection, still write it. Ask Him to show you the relationships.

Then pay attention to what you start thinking. Don't shut any of it out because you think it isn't important or because you don't want to think about that relationship because of the emotions attached to it. You won't have to relive these places over and over, but you do need to acknowledge it was wrong and has opened the door for the enemy to come into your life and steal from you. And if you have walked through this before maybe God is showing you something deeper to release to Him. Sometimes healing is in layers, as you can handle them.

Acknowledge each act of impurity with each specific individual. Even if your memory is pleasant because of the moment, but it was out of the marriage covenant, it has still stolen from you and from the other person—no matter what it feels like. There is still a soul tie that needs to be broken for you to give and receive fullness.

It is very important that you apply every part of your heart in being sorry for allowing it, whether you had given permission or not. Ask God to forgive you. Forgive others involved if it was pressured. Accept His forgiveness. Ask God to break every spiritual bond with that person. Then choose to repent, which means turn away from that relationship if you are still in it. If there are unrighteous actions with you and your spouse, I believe it is good to ask God to break unrighteous ties between you both now, and to break the generational curses of sex before marriage, so your children aren't set up to fail in that area. There are no guarantees as to what your children will choose, but if that stronghold is in place, there will be a strong desire to fulfill it that works against purity.

Wisdom

It is very important not to fly through this process; you need to hear God speaking to you in the midst, helping you in your healing. It is critical to take one person and one relationship at a time, naming each act of impurity specifically. This helps in taking full responsibility, acknowledging the impurity, and becoming free from each lingering spirit.

It is necessary to do this by separating each relationship. If the relationships have created other emotions such as hatred, anger, fear, disappointment, rejection, perversion, and or lust in you because of any offense, each place of emotion needs healing. It is important to forgive every offense so you can begin to work at releasing those emotions as well. Also, forgive yourself if you are experiencing anger or frustration towards yourself, and even forgive God if there may be that open door of disappointment, thinking God shouldn't have allowed it—rape or abuse.

The Truth is He has given humans the freedom to choose whom they will serve and how they will live, and then be responsible for the consequences of those actions.

God desires a people who will love Him and choose Him as He has chosen us. He will not treat us as robots, controlling every facet of life, nor do we desire that. His grace abounds so much that He grants us forgiveness even toward Himself. He doesn't need us to forgive Him, we need His forgiveness, yet sometimes we may have anger or unforgiveness towards Him because of our lack of understanding in what He allows.

I strongly encourage you *not* to just read through all of what I am sharing, but to apply every part of your heart if you want radical results.

> *Thank You, God, for revealing truth to me! I commit to You, I sit before You and bring all of these things in my life that You are pointing to right now and ask You to teach me, to show me what is truly pure in these situations. I want every spiritual tie broken with anything and anyone who is not pure, even if there are unhealthy spiritual ties with my spouse. I am coming to You with all of my heart in saying please forgive me for these relationships, for these covenants in my life. Thank You that Your blood covers all and breaks every bond. And after I walk through each relationship taking responsibility for them and how they have tainted my heart and my mind, I receive Your cleansing and I will try my best not to allow the enemy to condemn me or condemn myself for them any longer, for I understand this is Your grace.*

No matter how many names you have written, it is beneficial if you take the time to walk each relationship through the following cleansing, if you want complete freedom. This is well worth the time.

Please forgive me for the (emotional, sexual, and or spiritual) relationship I had with (specifically name). Forgive me for (name of specific acts). Please break every spiritual and emotional bond/tie with (name specific).

Continue applying each one on your list before moving on.

And if this applies:

Please forgive me for having sex (any form, even heavy petting) before I was married. Please break the generational curse of sex before marriage off of my heritage. Please forgive me for embracing the spirit of adultery. Will you break it off of me and my heritage? Thank You, Jesus, I am asking for what Your heart longs for, healing me and setting me free, so I rest in the fact that You are breaking through every stronghold for me.

And if this applies:

Please forgive me for opening the door to masturbation and/or pornography. Please break every bond with every individual I have lusted after. Forgive me for using them, pictures, or anything to satisfy myself and dishonoring them. Forgive me for trying to satisfy my own sexual cravings through my own body. Break the spirit of addiction and the generational curses of these spirits off of me and my family. Help me to run to You for those places of fulfillment. Help me to press into You for satisfaction of sensual desires. You will fill me in all my desires, whether supernaturally or through my spouse. Help me break all of these places of addictions. Show me what these counterfeits have hidden from me!

Father, I ask You to break every spirit of lust, perversion, fear, rejection, fear of being rejected, adultery, shame, guilt, condemnation, terror, any dirty spirit, addictions, pornography, masturbation...

(Listen for anything else God is speaking to break off—this can be perceived as a feeling, a vision, or a thought you remember).

Thank You, God. You are cleansing me from any spirits and all generational curses that have attached themselves to me through these relationships. You died to conquer these things in my life and I am grateful! I understand everything that has been stolen in my life is double portioned back to me. I believe You are opening this up to me. Restore all forms of true purity to me and my family. Let me guard and protect what You now entrust to me!

EXHORTATION

Ponder and celebrate in your heart what God has just done for you! Pay attention in the days ahead to how you see proof of change or how you feel different toward individuals or old relationships and how purity rises in you.

You may feel emotional, even physically lighter after praying through these prayers, many do; but even if you don't per se, feel anything, be at rest with all of it. You may just perceive greater joy and excitement toward your future and your marriage—that is what it is. It is important to address situations and sin in your life, but it is just as important *not* to live there. Rejoice in being set free and focus on pressing towards true ecstasy!

What you do not come in agreement with cannot manipulate you! If the enemy tries to steal any of this ground, you must stand firm and resist, and he will flee from you.[29] Believe; if you have set your heart to be free and your choice is greater purity, God will lead you out, purity and ecstasy will manifest in your life!

It truly is amazing to get healing just by having the right posture of our heart and accepting Christ's blood and His forgiveness. We cannot get true deliverance any other way. He has already done everything for us. We just need to walk in it! We really cannot explain deliverance and the fullness of the cross in words alone, but to experience freedom after we have been in bondage is a world of its own.

I know how it feels to be in extreme bondage and have Christ set me free. This freedom sets my heart on fire to want to know Him more. He is continually setting me free in my mindsets.

It's an awesome journey! And when you have tasted and walked in this joy, this ecstasy, you cannot help but to want others to experience it, too!

— 4 —

Two Ecstasy Killers

ENABLING

ENABLING can be positive or negative, depending on the motive and the intent behind it. We can enable others in positive ways that encourage them and enhance their strengths, or we can enable them in a negative way that hinders them from becoming who they were created to be, hindering them from rising to their full potential.

Enabling can be an ecstasy killer. Unless the enabling is coupled in Love, true Love, it will prevent us from moving in the fullness of our destiny!

I don't want to be responsible for hindering people from reaching their destiny. I think we should see and take responsibility for the adversity we may create in one another's lives.

Webster's Dictionary attributes enabling as giving power to, to make possible, to make easy, or to make ready to equip. Enabling of itself seems positive, yet if we attach it to insecurity of wanting people's approval or fear of losing our mate, it creates deep strongholds. Enabling will hinder fullness when we are giving power to negative affirmations, or making it possible for the mate to continue their criticisms and judgments, giving way for addictions.

Enabling is making provisions. We can make provisions for our spouse to mistreat us by not handling it properly, being inactive in our response. We are enabling if we allow emotional, physical, even spiritual abuse.

Yes, it is wrong to walk in these abuses, but I believe it is just as wrong to submit to them, enabling them. I am not saying to get up and leave your marriage if this is your situation. I believe there are ways that God leads you through to break these cycles if both are willing.

There are many avenues of enabling. Enabling is positive if it accents positive standards. We can enable each other in accomplishing great tasks by making way for them, encouraging them to come forth. This is how we want to enable.

Anytime where I have seen instances of enabling that had created unhealthy cycles, even if there was a desire for better, the motive or root momentum was always negative. I have yet to see the end result turn out well from this type of enabling; it feeds on the negative sources, unless the person chooses to stop the cycle.

I knew a woman who was married to an alcoholic, and she would borrow money from her adult children to buy her husband beer. She didn't like that he drank all of the time, but she lived in fear that he would leave her, so she tried to give him everything he wanted. She continued in this negative-enabling pattern and neither she nor her husband ever received good fruit as the end result. Sadly, she couldn't see any other way to handle the situation. Her fear was so great that she actually enabled and gave power to what she hated.

Not all times, but many times, we walk in the same enabling that was displayed during our youth. Sometimes it is easier to see someone else's situation as unhealthy behavior before we realize the unhealthy cycles of our own. Nonetheless, if you ask God to show you and you are willing to walk in whatever it takes to be free, He will lead the way. I say to walk in whatever it takes because there is usually a cost to break every stronghold. There is usually a laying down of something (selfishness, pride, control, fear) when we have walked for so long one way—it becomes comfortable, whether it is right or wrong. But the cost is nothing when compared to the peace, joy, and ecstasy that you will attain!

The Lord opened my eyes years ago to how I was enabling my husband in a couple different ways. I always felt that I should pull my weight in all things in our marriage, and that meant physically as well as financially, paralleling myself to my husband.

As we were building our first house, my husband and I were carrying 12 inch cement blocks from the edge of the property to the foundation. Well, if my husband carried four at a time, then I needed to carry at least two. I didn't assume I needed to do as much, but to do all I could. And maybe that wasn't so bad. But when it came to digging the sump pump, all day long I dug with an pickaxe. In extreme pain in my body and with blisters on my hand, I refused to hand it over to him. I could do it. After all, he was building the rest of the house. This was the least I could do. I thought this was a strength, and maybe to some degree it was. It wasn't until several years later that my eyes were opened, and I started searching my heart for ways I was enabling any negative empowerment that could destroy our relationship, or taint it.

I began seeing in myself an *I can take care of myself* attitude. I appreciated my husband and his strength and wisdom, but, well, if he ever decided to leave, I could take care of myself. I didn't fully need him. Wow! What an independent, prideful spirit. God wants us to be strong, but that is over the top. I had realized that my actions were displaying my subconscious thinking in the fact that I was let down so many times in life that I didn't want to be hurt again. I was being so strong I was actually not recognizing the greater gifts of strength that were in my husband because I disenabled them from coming forth.

It is not always about what we do, but the motive of our heart in doing it. In allowing my heart to be broken open and releasing these wrong spirits of independency and pride, I saw that the root of them for me was fear, the fear of being left alone, abandoned. I was making sure, subconsciously, that I could still make it. I had to deal with that fear, which is a lie that I believed.

The truth is, there are no guarantees that our mates will stay with us and be faithful; but, God will always be with us and remain faithful. Moving in what He desires brings fulfillment and abundance in our lives. If our lives change up because of choices that are made, God will still be all that He is and ever will be. The visions for our lives could be altered because of the decisions we or our spouses make, but the calls on our lives won't. God's dreams of fulfillment will not let up!

As I have surrendered my independent attitude and backed up in seeing what I am supposed to be doing, I have found a whole new level of adoring my husband's strength. I have seen as I have pulled back, he rose up in the rightful place. I was preventing him from experiencing fullness as well as benefiting from it myself. His strength, now, is even a new place of romance in thought for me.

In marriage, it is first an individual decision to walk away from unhealthy cycles, and then hopefully a united force comes in agreement to diminish them. It is amazing and wonderful when both husband and wife are eager, honest, and willing to do whatever it takes to disarm unhealthy cycles. It is to improve their marriage initially, but the agreement also improves their future, their strength, and deposits value in their heritage that only increases by their choices for more.

So often we just believe that it is what it is—mountains of problems in our lives. The Truth is, through Christ we have the power to change and be delivered within ourselves, from every stronghold.

Yet many succumb to what they are dealt because they don't realize they were made for so much more. They may recognize the Truth, they prayed once about it and felt nothing happened so they just accept what is, as if it is meant to be. This should not be so.

If we are believing, pressing, contending for circumstances to change and or healing whether for ourselves or for others, many times it may be asking more than once, till we break through even in our own believing. It's not because God needs to hear it more than once, I believe we need to hear it, speak it and press through in the believing for the supernatural to manifest.

We are truly more than conquerors![30] Do we believe that? We were created to move mountains with faith as small as a mustard seed, a smidge of believing.[31] We can break every chain within our own entanglements by believing and walking through it with the Lord. I will emphasize again, it is believing, without proof, and walking it out as it will be. But we cannot force our mates to choose it or want it themselves. This is where it gets more intense for some. If we don't have full unity in faith where we are going in the journey, and are at completely different levels or places, it is still not impossible. It simply requires more faith, more trusting, more leaning not on our own understanding.[32]

Most couples I know are not spiritually at the same place. I don't believe it is healthy to hold back progressing in your faith because your spouse is not at the same place of understanding spiritually. I don't believe that is God's intent for us personally, or as a couple.

I will say this as well for some who need to hear the encouragement by it: as a wife I am more vocal and more intense and visual in my walk with God and everyday life. My husband is more conservative. He may not go barreling out in all directions, but if I want to pray, he will agree with me in it. We are individuals, yet we are one in our marriage. I do not think God calls us to make sure we move together in the same levels of faith or places, waiting on the other before we progress. I think we are to spur each other on, not to compete nor compare. I do believe that it is vital to honor and respect each other wherever we are in the journey.

It takes courage to look at our behaviors. It takes courage to take responsibility and choose to stop the cycle, whether it is choosing to stop feeding the things that are killing your relationship, or to stop *expecting* or receiving from your mate the things that contribute to destruction. This takes great maturity either way to see it for what it is, and commit to not being manipulated by it anymore. This leads us to the second ecstasy killer~ unrealistic expectations.

EXPECTATIONS

Expectations can be blatant, outright. Expectations can also be unspoken, assumed. Expectations can be a great help to one another in our agreement of how we take responsibility for accomplishing tasks in the home or business. It is a healthy understanding and not a rule.

It is the unrealistic expectations that kill ecstasy. They are a heavy weight of pressure and they are not realistic when we are learning to adapt to Love.

Outright expectations in a marriage are ones you express to each other; for instance, you discuss how the house responsibilities will be handled, how you expect to be treated, how many children you would like to have, financial strategies, material desires… the substances of life together. Some of these expectations change over time, so couples need to continually communicate their hearts to one another.

On the other hand, many times expectations are unspoken or assumed. It is a mindset we accept as the only way, good or bad. We accepted it growing up watching our parents, or lack thereof, drawing our own conclusions. Or, we made a decision in our minds one day about how things should be and then we lived it out, not realizing the damage it created in our relationships.

For example, it was right after our fourth child was born. Physically for me, it was a lot to handle: not sleeping at night, home schooling, working, and adjusting the family to our new addition. Having the gift of four girls and being able to be home with them is one of the greatest gifts God has poured out over me, right after giving me an amazing man for a husband. Even in the midst of blessings there are sometimes adjustments that I didn't know were coming. I somehow had this idea, that since my husband went to work all day, I should do everything in and around the house. Superwoman, right? It was never spoken or agreed on, I just assumed it.

One afternoon I was standing in line at check out. It had been three and a half hours since we left the house with a forty minute drive to get there. I had all four girls with me. I had to stop to breast feed twice in the store while shopping to try to keep moving. My two year-old started screaming to get out of the cart because she had been there for a while and she is hungry now too. My six and seven year-olds were also tired of shopping at this point.

We finally made it to the van and I called my husband in despair, *Please don't ever let me, with a newborn, take all four children grocery shopping by myself.* His response, *I never asked you to do that yourself; I would have helped you if you would have waited.*

I was speechless. I thought I was supposed to do all of that. I wanted to have everything done at the house, groceries bought, supper cooked before he returned home from work so he could relax. This was my heart motive, that he could come home and rest. That doesn't seem wrong in and of itself, yet in doing this God started showing me I was hindering Steve from becoming who God was calling him to be as a father and as a husband. I was all but killing myself so he could rest, not loving myself in the process. I had put expectations on myself that were unrealistic, and I was disenabling him to rise in the responsibilities. So I began to pull back and ask my husband for help. It was awkward at first, as if I was asking of him too much.

I can see it was pride also to think, "I can do it all myself." It took the fourth child to be fully enlightened. Some may get it with two children, it took me four. For some of us it takes a little more to see.

It also took me coming to the place where I said, *I can't do this all myself,* to ask God for help in greater places, and to see the way that He wanted me to let Him help was through Steve. I had been praying for years for our marriage and unity, and for God to bring us where He wanted, not realizing how deep the changes were going to be and what was going to be exposed through the process. It was good! It wasn't easy, but it has brought such freedom and oneness in sharing the gift of being what each other needs at every angle.

We are still progressing as I hope we always will, because oneness doesn't stop; I believe it only gets better and deeper!

Here again my true heart motive wasn't fully wrong. I felt I was to contribute as much as I could, but in the midst I had also recognized that I subconsciously was thinking I had to prove, validate, or protect myself from getting hurt. Strangely, I had never seen that in myself before, that I somehow needed to validate myself in the marriage. If I had known my worth in

Christ, I wouldn't have needed to prove myself worthy. It goes back to the motive, because you could take the same actions with a pure motive and not get the same response in the end.

So, if one spouse is negatively enabling in the relationship, how does it get exposed? We need to first understand that we want all things hidden to be revealed for our own freedom, because secrets only keep us in bondage.

Hidden, secret things keep us from embracing deeper
levels of intimacy with God and our mate.

Simply asking God to expose any places of enabling will release these barriers; but, after we ask God for truth, we then need to pay attention to what happens next. God is speaking and He wants us to live in freedom, more than we do! As we perceive truth, we need to take responsibility for it and make the changes towards becoming Love. Our greatest quest is to work on adapting ourselves to Love. We can only ever change ourselves and then trust God with the rest. This alone creates more peace and joy!

In marriage especially, sometimes we have ideas, theories, and plans about what we personally want and expect to get out of our marital relationship. And sometimes we are so focused on *our* expectations, we miss the whole point of what God desires and what fullness He wants to release in us, which is far greater.

Each one of us was made for greatness, then, to come into unity with one another, to bring greatness into two lives, believing, pushing every obstacle out of the way, and bringing fullness.

I am convinced from what I see in marriages around me, that many are not experiencing fullness in their marriage. They're settling for less because they don't know that there is so much more. Again, I am not professing to you perfection in marriage, but excellence, trying our best, inviting God and moving with Him in it.

We can have obvious expectations like expecting our mates to be nice. We may think another obvious expectation is for our spouses to clean up after themselves, therefore working as a team. Some think obvious expectations are for the woman to do all the inside work and the man to do all the outside work, regardless if both have full-time jobs.

Then there are the hidden expectations, the assumptions you have without ever conversing about them. It may be as you have always seen it done when you were growing up, or it is how you always dreamed marriage would be—and you *assume* your mate knows and wants this same dream. It may be a certain way you want to be held or kissed. It may be the way you want your mate to greet you at the door. It may be the way you want your mate to back you up in honor and respect, with spoken or unspoken words, when adversity comes into view, with your children, friends, or strangers.

I believe, whether we want to accept it or not, all of these spoken and unspoken, realistic and unrealistic expectations affect the depth of our true intimacy with each other. They affect the depth of ecstasy we can attain and walk in.

Every detail of belief and perception of each other, the amount of support or lack of it that we feel is all relative. The only way to get where we desire to go in fullness and in ecstasy is to observe the reality that is moving in our lives, take responsibility, and shift our beliefs in Love. Take time to think about what you really desire, encourage your mate to do the same, and share that with each other—understanding, and not expecting it all to be accomplished in one afternoon.

As we share our hearts, we can help each other see what the other perceives in what the fullness really is, and then move toward it. This is extremely enlightening! I still do this with my spouse after twenty-six years and still find interesting new insights as to what he enjoys. We also have changed our minds on what we desired initially.

My husband made a comment fifteen years ago that every morning we were camping, he wanted to eat bacon and eggs. I accommodated him for many years until my desire for cooking it, and eating that breakfast every camping vacation, was no longer any form of joy. I chose to do what I thought a great wife would do and cooked it anyway. One particular morning, he said he wasn't hungry after I said that breakfast was ready. I was, to say the least, livid. That may seem like a very small, even minute issue, but in that moment it was Mount Everest!

I went for a run and conversed with the Lord about what the real issue was. Then I realized I felt *expected* to make the bacon and eggs because he asked for it years ago and I had a strong desire to please him. It was an expectation I had put on myself. When I returned to our campsite and sat down to share my heart, to him it was no big deal. He said, *I don't ever remember saying that fifteen years ago. You don't have to make it if you don't want to. If I want it, I will cook it myself.* He shares all of this with absolutely no attitude. This was amazing to me that he doesn't really want me to do things for him that I don't want to do. I needed to hear that for myself and see his heart to allow that expectation to completely diminish.

If I would have shared my change in heart when I started noticing it, I would have found out that he had changed his mind in what he desired as well. Amazing how some things are orchestrated in our lives, not by accident, and if we just communicate better we can save ourselves a lot of heartache and frustration!

We may also have expectations in what we find appealing in our mate's physical appearance, such as maintaining a healthy weight, teeth, smelling good, and wearing nice clothes; yet, we do not always share these outright thoughts with our mates. We assume they know, like it is common sense. But honestly, it could be life-altering for our marriage to ask the questions or share our heart about what we desire; not to compare with others, but our personal desires for them that attract us.

Some people suffer with depression; and if so, as it intensifies they many times, get to the point where they struggle with getting out of bed, taking showers, taking care of themselves, and loving themselves.

If we see these things happening, we need to speak truth as to what we desire and share what appeals to each one of us personally. Pray and break-through the depression together. We may have to address these issues several times to help them, but if we truly love them, we will lovingly present the truth.

Wisdom is to acknowledge and bring to light what perspectives are unhealthy and how we enable them, and then, choose to go in the direction that brings Love.

Here are a few perspectives to consider: If a spouse makes comments about an actor or actress that they find appealing in a movie, it sends an unspoken expectation to the other mate that they ought to be like that to be appealing. It can set up unrealistic expectations. If they are married to a mate who is very insecure and thinks he or she is unattractive, this can cause even greater insecurities because the spouse thinks they will never measure up to that standard.

Though your mate may be secure in who he or she is, it still opens the door to lust when you allow your mind to linger on people long enough to affirm any attraction to them.

Some people feel it is harmless because they most likely will never connect with someone famous, so it is safe to lust after or make comments. I disagree. If we compare, we set our spouse up to feel inadequate or inferior. Some get so stimulated by others they do not realize what that circumstance creates that is negatively affecting their ability to embrace true ecstasy.

There is a fine line between having an appreciation for beauty in purity and crossing the line of impurity into lust that hinders fullness in our life. Some cannot define the line between the two because of the gates that have been opened to lust in their hearts. When there is a lusting after other individuals outside of marriage, there will be disappointment. There is always going to be a let-down, no matter how good it is perceived to be and the ability to be content and fulfilled will not be experienced—killing ecstasy!

I knew a married woman who would openly speak how *hot* other men were. When I commented that I could not believe she would say that even in front of her husband (my heart ached for him), her response was, *My husband knows I would never cheat on him.* She thought it was harmless, but years later she found that her husband had been sleeping with another woman.

She may have thought it was harmless, and I do not condone his actions, but I do strongly feel that all of our affection and adorations should be for our mates. That may or may not have changed circumstances, but I feel we need to be sensitive to our mate's needs and not open doors of rejection that may lead to adultery.

If our minds are here or there, not focused on actively pursuing Love, we may miss an awesome opportunity to create ecstasy and passion with our spouse. To attain true ecstasy we cannot make any provision for impurity. The choice is always ours.

You will not ever taste the realm of ecstasy and purity in your marriage and think afterward that you wished you would have allowed room for distractions. There is no comparison.

> *I thank You, Lord. You are calling us higher in our marriages and You will reward those who are diligent to purify themselves more and more greatly, for You are pure. To those who are pure, You will reveal Yourself pure. As we are being vulnerable in looking deeper into our hearts and motives, we want You to expose and bring light in every place of hindrance.*
>
> *Will You show us any and all ways that we may be enabling one another or having expectations? Show us healthy enabling so we can praise You and be thankful for it, as well as unhealthy enabling so we can take responsibility to break the chains through You and grow in positive directions. Shed light on the expectations we have and help us to affirm them if they are aligned in who we are destined to be. And if there is any place of conflict in these expectations, help us to surrender it to You and trust You in bringing us to unity.*
>
> *Open our eyes, our hearts, our ears, and our minds to accept truth about ourselves. Give us the diligence to press into the uncomfortable and break every unhealthy and unrealistic expectation, bringing us to greater love, greater unity, greater communication, and understanding.*

Thank You; for Your Word says if we come to You, humble ourselves and pray, and turn from our selfish ways, You will come and heal our land[33] (every part of who we are and destined to become). Thank You; for You teach us how to pray and always give us greater hope for our future. What more can we ask? We are humbled that You love us this much! Thank You for always moving in, through, and around us!

– 5 –

Authentic Love

Now that we are purposely becoming more aware of what kills ecstasy and what love is not, let us evolve towards what real Love is. Authentic Love is strong, foundational, and unmovable. True ecstasy is enraptured *only* in authentic real Love.

AUTHENTIC LOVE SEES AND BELIEVES

I choose to believe the Word and practice seeing what God sees in my husband and speak it forth. My mindsets have changed because I am allowing the Word to move in my life because I am making room for it in believing. I am more at peace, experience more joy, and I am sure I have to be a lot more fun to be married to than before because it has proven itself effective. I used to be unsettled, anxious, untrusting, and very insecure. Now I choose to believe who God says I am and what I am created for and likewise, I am believing greatness for and towards my husband.

To practice seeing as God sees as well as practice believing what He speaks is crucial to ongoing encouragement as well as progressing through intensities in life. Seeing and believing in every part of your life can be challenging, but it will change your life incredibly.

Speaking and believing for greater, may be the exact opposite of what is coming out of your spouse in the moment. It is vital in continuing to practice believing as you wait on God. Be content to wait as long as it takes. Again, I will say as long as it takes. Then obey what He tells you to do. This is truly what believing is. You cannot quit speaking or believing even if what you desire hasn't manifested yet. This is when the true testing comes. There may be several things that He may ask you to do to encompass your believing. If it is in the arena of finances, for some He may speak about tithing; and for others, it may be to look for a job. It is very important to believe, stand, and move with Him in every place. This is where satisfaction comes even while you wait.

If you ever have to wait on God, it is because
you need strength for the next thing.[34]

We are to call things that are not, as though they were.[35] Call them the way God sees them, as the way He desired from the beginning. This is the power of the spoken Word.

For example, you think that your finances are not enough to pay your bills. You are being faithful with working as much as you can. You try to be diligent in inviting God to help you, as you continue to tithe with the right heart. You are trying not to spend frivolously, and yet there is not enough. Call the situation how God sees it and watch it change. Believe that the finances are there and that God will provide for all your needs. He will! It may not be recognizable how it happens, and all you can say is somehow all of the bills are getting paid.

To practice believing in finances may look like this: speaking to your finances to multiply, purposely believing that God is multiplying, reminding yourself, and saying *I have more than enough.*

If you ever get to a place where you feel you have hit a wall within yourself and lost hope, it is important to go back again to the Word, to God's heart on the subject and speak it again, (write it down, whatever it takes) what you know and hope, until you rise in believing again. It is critical to learn how to encourage yourself, but also to hear God trying to encourage you. If your ears aren't trained in believing, it will be hard to hear Him at first because that is what He speaks. Be sensitive to hear God in the prophetic, whether it's His heart and vision over your mate, or it's how to embrace more wisdom in spending and/or other life challenges.

Decree a thing and it will be established (Job 22:28 NKJV).

Speak into existence what you do not see manifesting that is righteous and good! This is just agreeing with God, making way for it to come forth. If God is Love, then isn't it righteous to ask and agree with God for those fruits of Love to come to maturity in each other?

There are some things that have not come into existence in our lives yet, but come into existence by the prophetic Word, which God is speaking forth into existence through us.

> *You have heard [these things foretold], now you see this fulfillment. And will you not bear witness to it? I show you specified new things from this time forth, even hidden things [kept in reserve] which you have not known. There are created now [called into being by the prophetic word], and not long ago; and before today you have never heard of them, lest you should say, Behold, I knew them!* (Isaiah 48:6-7 AMP)

This Word can release an excitement and anticipation all on Its own! Just to think that God has hidden things just for us to agree with Him and watch it happen in our lives![36]

See it, believe it, and speak it!

AUTHENTIC LOVE SPEAKS LIFE

How do I speak authentic Love into my husband? I write notes and put them in his lunchbox or I will text him saying, *You are a mighty man of valor! You walk in strength and integrity. You are amazing! Thank you for marrying me. Thank you for coming home to me. Thank you for working so hard to provide for our family! Thank you for fixing everything that breaks around here! Thank you for protecting and looking out for me!* I tell him how attractive he is! I want my husband to have the words of his heart spoken through his wife. I want to be every bit of the helpmate I was created to be. I want to be that place of building up for him to affirm him in who he is. Just yesterday I was getting a glimpse of the creativity that is locked up inside him, so I told him what I saw and I want to help encourage him to release it.

What is really amazing, as well, is that as he has experienced the blessing of hearing edifying truth about himself, it is building his confidence and he has started to sow the same seeds in me. What an encouragement! My motive isn't to build him up so he will build me up, though it is great when it comes back around.

If we are motivated out of Love, we speak encouragement to our mates just to build them up. It is not about what we gain. It is about what we can give. In the midst of the right heart and motive, we begin to reap our heart's desires!

Someone else's spouse may come to mind and you may think, *Sure, it's easy to speak that about them. They are an amazing husband/wife.* The truth is, we are all made uniquely and are all gifted. We are all seen amazingly by God, so we just need to connect with God's perspective about our mate and appreciate them for who they are.

I started speaking Love to my husband before I could fully see it. I was only getting glimpses of it. I didn't realize at first that these glimpse were actually Papa speaking and revealing truth to me.

I would even tell my husband if I couldn't see parts of him healed in glimpses, then I would just accept what I saw on the forefront of his person as being his fullest. But those glimpses helped me to believe for the greatest…and continue to do so!

As I began to see what healing looked like in my husband, I wanted it all! It caused me to pray more, believe more, and encourage him more in it. When I first started encouraging him in what God was showing me of what He wanted to heal, it was unusual because I wasn't used to doing it. Something as simple as Papa releasing greater joy in replacing abrasiveness that continually would steal from my husband. I didn't see it or feel it 100 percent in my being. Only God could bring this healing, I just chose to see it, believe it, and then speak it till I *could* see it! It was and is only by faith that I see something greater, a glimmer. I do not have proof of greatness. I have God's Spirit speaking in me and showing me how to believe and pray. Then I walk it out!

My husband and I have walked through a whole lot of hardship and pain. We are *in the process* of healing as we all are somewhere in this journey of life. I have been several times at complete brokenness, emptiness, and pain. I have been so numb that I didn't have stirred emotions of love. It has not ever been through any purposed fault of my husband. I have come to realize that I was too focused on wanting my husband to meet my needs and desires instead of God fulfilling me.

We are mere beings, imperfect at best on our own. We cannot meet every need and desire of each other on our own. We were created from the beginning to have God walk right with us through all things.

I cannot be the wife my husband needs, or desires, in and of myself. I need to be anchored to the One who will equip me in all things in true Love, to the One who will show me how to touch and talk to my husband that brings the greatest fullness for him, for us.

I see now that my purpose is to have my focus on God—Authentic Love—and get filled up by Him and then pour into my husband. It has taken me a long journey to figure this out, but has been well worth the revelation. I need to walk in a continued posture of awareness. This isn't some place to arrive at, but rather a consistent daily goal to achieve.

If our focus is on another human being, we will be disappointed because we are flesh and we make a lot of mistakes; but, if we align ourselves in Christ, we can be the mate we are called to be for each other without false expectations. It is true the emotions of Love are secondary. After we choose to walk in the attributes of Love, emotions will come as we process through them.

Authentic Love Trusts

If we have had Love modeled to us growing up, we have so much more than what we realize. And if our mates did not, it takes a lot more patience and love being manifested in them to believe the goals of Love in marriage and to learn to trust as Love trusts, wholeheartedly.

God equips and gives you exactly everything you need, but it is in Him in you; some things are released as you are more in Him and can rest to have it release. It is easier to hear Him when you can rest. For some the very word rest is obsolete, null and void. I encourage you to go after rest and peace!

It is not by accident that our bodies heal when we are resting them. It is not by accident that God asks us to rest on the Sabbath; and scientifically, the moon's weekly alignment affects our bodies in healing if we are resting them in it. There is something that happens in stillness, we learn to know who He is.

Are we speaking Truth or speaking facts? The Truth is God's heart and desires that may not have manifested yet. The facts are what are manifesting right now, on the forefront, that are not the fullness of our destiny.

Some may say in the midst of heartache, *I am only speaking truth. He is a jerk.* Truth is, he may be acting like a jerk in the moment, but to call him one only criticizes his heart and character and affirms his choices of actions. As a person thinks in his heart, so he is. So if you think and speak that he is, it will be hard to ever see anything more rise in him.

Sometimes we have acted like jerks ourselves. Well, I can only speak for myself, and I would never have wanted my husband to call me one or think I was being one. As we judge, we too will be judged. If we judge and discern in Love, we sow those seeds to come back in Love. If we aren't building our spouses up, we are tearing them down. There is no between.

Recognizing Truth is to see humanity's perspectives are not God's perspective. If we are truly entrusted with each other's hearts, which I believe we are, to be successful with them, we must see them in Truth.

This is something the Lord spoke to me when I was at one of the most broken, wounded place of pain; as I looked at my husband the Lord spoke, *I have entrusted you with his heart!* It is seriously amazing how one Word from God will change your perspective, the course of your heart and life in a moment, if you are open to receive It! Aspiring this Authentic Love is the highest place!

Being trusted, trusting each other, and speaking Truth are extremely intertwined. The power of life and death is in the tongue and if you desire to speak life into your mate, you will speak what God's heart is seeing in them. You will call out what God wants to move through them.

I believe this can speed up the process of us receiving the Truth of who we are, by someone speaking and believing it about us. It is the same thing if we speak over a child as he is growing up that he is a failure and he will never make it. This is a great hindrance for him to know who he really is and live a life of success. He can do it once he is able to receive healing and disarm the lies he heard about himself. Success is always there because of God's plan for his life, but he has trouble connecting with it.

There are many people who have these issues because no one ever spoke life in and over them. It is power released whether we choose to speak and think negatively or positively.

God has made us in His image. He has brought everything into being by His speaking it forth. Therefore He has given us that same authority with speaking and the power released in it. *If anything would cause the fear of the Lord in us, may it be to recognize this power and purpose to only build up what is good and tear down what is evil.* For as we truly get and live this revelation, the Kingdom of God advances, displaying more peace and joy. We cannot experience the power of the Word if we don't step out and exercise and test its strengths.

What do I mean? I am saying to exercise the Word is to speak it, eat it, (meditate and process it), believe it, let it become in you, and wait on it to prove itself. Test it!

Authentic Love Resurrects

I have felt many times that part of Stephanie had died. I want to encourage you if you are relating to what I am sharing. God wants to heal every part of your heart and marriage. I believe that the first "raising of the dead" we ought to do is raising every fragmented part of our own heart from the dead. Command it back to life. I do not believe God ever desires any part of our hearts to die from any process of this life, because all things work for our good.[37]

I will say this as well, if you are in pain or feel dead inside because of ongoing disappointments, I do not believe any loving spouse purposes to destroy another or create pain. Choose to believe Love—the best.

Sometimes spouses can get caught up in revenge or selfishness, but most times when you get into the heart of their hearts, they don't want to hurt anyone. They are just reacting to the pain in their heart or just trying to function through the pain. Revenge does not ever reveal any form of Love or Peace. Many times we hurt each other with very little effort.

I encourage you to stop right now and analyze your life, your heart, and your dreams. Do you feel your dreams have died because of your spouse's choices? Do you feel that you have let go of believing because you are continually disappointed with the outcome? Have you lost yourself in your ploy to fulfill your mate's desires? The best thing you can ever admit to yourself is that you see where you have died in your perceptions or your passions. The Truth is you probably will not get healed until you see your need to be healed. It is part of accepting Truth and taking responsibility; being awakened to your true destiny, which is the abundant life that Christ sacrificed to give you.

If you cannot see any part of your heart that has died initially, maybe you are at a good place right now and that is awesome!

It is wisdom to recognize that we may not always see clearly for ourselves; at times it is because we aren't sensitive in some areas of our hearts. These are places only God Himself can reveal and walk us through. I don't think we should let up in any direction of pressing for healing until we are living life outrageously and abundantly. Life abundantly is recognizing and experiencing the Spirit of God moving in all, and every weakness, making His strength perfect in us.[38] It's a life of living and knowing impossibilities made possible. It is receiving and living in over-abundant hope, peace, joy, and Love.

I believe raising ourselves from the dead is what may be our first experience of resurrection. Though we are not physically dead, being emotionally or spiritually dead is just as tragic.

"Hope deferred makes the heart sick" (Proverbs 13:12 NKJV). To maintain hope is to maintain healing. Hope deferred can open the door for depression (which is suppressed anger a lot of times), oppression, resentment, bitterness, even suicide, sickness, and disease. Sometimes the pain can be so intense that you can't see where hope is or was lost, you may not know what to hope for anymore. This is what is so awesome about the greatness of God. He has given you all authority through Christ. You believe and agree with Him in this and exercise it. You command every part of your heart to be resurrected in the name of Jesus and He does it. He moves in this for you. You command everything that has been stolen to be restored *double* back to you, for this is your heritage in Christ.[39]

What outrageousness would begin to happen if we took this seriously and stood on it?

We commit to begin believing for fullness and oneness again, because He says no good thing will He withhold from those whose walk is upright.[40] It is a choice to walk in every place of righteousness; and if we do, we then can expect goodness to surround us. This doesn't mean ease and perfection. It means strengthened, empowered, directed, purposed, and promised. He has given us everything we need in Him for success, but we still have to do our part in choosing every part of Love (Him) to manifest in us and through us—letting go of every offense, forgiving every disappointment, and believing that God will redeem everything somehow, some way.

⁕

I believe it is possible that many of our marital problems can be processed and resolved more quickly and even lead us to personal and marital ecstasy if we take the time to see them as part of our purpose. Here again if the goal is to personally grow in and be love, this alone helps quicken the process because we are purposely working on being love, hoping that your mate is doing the same in every hard place and struggle.

I see this in my own marriage. As we are making active choices, issues progress more quickly and more joy is released because we know the mountain of adversity is going to move and is moving~ eyes of faith, believing. I see it in the lives of family and friends who choose to purpose to live Love. I also see this concept work in other marriages when I share with couples what God keeps teaching me and then they appropriate their hearts to Love.

Not all problems resolve quickly. Some situations take years of working together, lots of prayer (inviting God into it, listening for His wisdom we are to walk into, in the moment), and choosing Love. Yet even so, nowhere in the process do we ever have to negate peace as we are working through them.

I believe if we are disciplined in our focus and adapt as God points to our hearts, a lot of issues can be quickly resolved. They are not resolved because we get our own way or because the adversity is eliminated, but problems are resolved by choosing God's way. Choosing to forgive, choosing to be Love—believing the best of our mates and believing for greater in the outcome. This positions us for ecstasy.

If just one in the relationship chooses to start a right cycle, God will honor the efforts; but again, we are in this for the long haul. We don't want to allow unbelief (thinking that resolution isn't going to happen) at any point or allow ourselves to get discouraged. We have to believe God is greater and He is moving in us the moment we invited Him. Encouragement from Him continues as we continue to invite Him—Love—and align our hearts with His.

I am one who does not like to go around the same mountain twice; meaning, I do not like to revisit the same issues in my life over and over just because I am being too hard headed to "get it." I believe God allows us to go through reoccurrences so we get the principles in life to help us.

He loves us that much to be that thorough. That is how much He wants us to achieve fullness. Some may think it's a curse, but it is Love helping us to progress in Him.

Maturing into Love is just as important as when we were in elementary school and learning to read, write, and understand arithmetic, the building blocks of learning. If we skip any concept at all, it causes everything else to be a stumbling here and there while we are trying to learn more; therefore, we cannot effectively progress into our full potential, which is the core of life in learning and communications. We are handicapped, academically. Likewise, until we learn a marriage relationship based in Love, we are handicapped, until we get healing.

To learn all of the true concepts of love and apply each of them to our hearts at every precipice moment is to make steady progression. Because we are destined to be Love and become Love, if we desire to progress as quickly as possible it creates more peace and joy in the midst. God promises His people that He makes their feet advance and progress and not slip as they trust in His strength to bring them through.

> The Lord God is my Strength, my personal bravery, and my invincible army; **He makes my feet** like hinds feet and will make me to **walk [not to stand still in terror, but to walk] and make [spiritual] progress upon my high places [of trouble, suffering, or responsibility]!** (Habakkuk 3:19 AMP)

Because God is your strength, He causes you to continue to progress in hard places, in places of fear, in places of trouble, or responsibility. You are not at a standstill, no matter what it looks like. You are constantly moving, constantly progressing! If you focus on circumstances, the fear that arises can paralyze you; but, if you keep your heart and mind steadfast on Him, He will keep you in perfect peace.[41] This is a moment to moment discipline we learn.

Allow God to open, even now, more of His heart in you.

The awesome part of Papa is that we are constantly progressing in revelation. There is always room to mature and grow. This is why it is extremely important to keep our hearts humble, moldable, and teachable; otherwise, we will miss attaining more depth of understanding and insight of His heart, of Love.

The enemy would love for us to believe that we continue to go around the same tree over and over again, not progressing or changing. He would love for us to believe that we are caught in failure and that we will live there indefinitely. This is not so. We are constantly progressing in our journey with the Lord, and we have to progress in believing the best, even of ourselves, to attain stability in our walk.

It doesn't matter what your situation is, in Christ, you are in Him, He is in you. If you have your heart postured to try your best in walking with Him and obeying, then the Truth is, you are constantly progressing, not being perfect, but trying for excellence! You may perceive the same situation, but He makes your feet like hinds feet, causing you to stick to the edge of the cliff, not allowing your feet to slip, and you are *progressing through all* your places of trouble. Be encouraged!

As God is your strength, He causes you to be firm in your progressions of fullness in your destiny. If you are reading this and you know you haven't been walking in obedience to God, or you haven't been obedient to what you know is right, it's not too late. Get up and go again. Make it right. There is no greater time. Accept the grace given to you right now! You are the one missing out!

If there is so much promise over, in, and around us, why would we choose any other way or accept anything else? Everything else leaves you void and empty after the height of the moment. We were created in Him and for Him, so it makes logical sense why we will not touch fullness, oneness, or true ecstasy, apart from Him.

Walking with Papa is an unbroken, daily decision we all make. For me, I need Him. That is not something I just say. It is not false humility either. I have fallen on my face allot in life doing life Stephanie's way—making a mess of everything that surrounded me at the time. I hope I do not ever forget where I have been so I can always remember what He brought me out of! I don't want to fall on my face anymore. I want the greatest, and I know I cannot achieve it apart from Him, because greatness is Him. This doesn't mean that I don't make mistakes. It means I am trying not to fight God anymore about who is in the driver's seat. I have already seen what life looks like from that viewpoint, and it is not pretty, I've been there done that. I hope Wisdom has a full grip on me so I do not ever feel the need to revisit that mindset again.

I'm bringing humor, but seriously, this is the battle of every believer at the core, to submit and let God bring forth His Kingdom out of you, your finest! His Kingdom is the height of Wisdom and Success in you! Christ in you, the Hope of glory.

Authentic Love Searches for Wisdom

If I say that finding Wisdom, for me, started in tattling to Papa, it sounds childish, doesn't it? In my home, while growing up, it was not ever accepted to tattletale. Yet, when I contemplate my actions and behaviors of what I was doing, I don't know what else to call it. The child who is running to the adult to expose what is wrong in a situation may have several different motives, but most times it is to either vindicate themselves or try to invoke revenge, or both.

To Tattletale to Papa is a much better stepping stone to maturity rather than to trash your husband or wife to any or all who are around you in the moment of friction. You cannot erase from people's minds after you have spoken negative about your mate, though you may have already moved onto forgiveness and healing. People do not forget, so those negative condemnations always stick, causing ill emotions that you, at some point will regret them thinking.

Most of us can not keep quiet when we are head to head with our mate, so who do we talk to when we are frustrated? It is very natural to want to share our hearts and verbalize the frustrations with someone not directly connected, as we look for the resolve. I think sometimes, however, we are looking for someone to just agree that we are right and our mate is wrong, or just to have someone relate to our heart.

So who do you run to when you are hurting or upset? God? Your best friend? Your family? Who is greater and most wise? This question is to only bring awareness—not to condemn.

Sometimes we do not realize the cycles we embrace.

Well…maybe I'll just call my best friend Ginger because I can trust her. In fact, I tell her everything. I share so much that I spend more time talking to her than my husband. Well, I need to talk to someone right? And God's opinions…well, I know He doesn't appreciate my husband talking to me like that. I already know what He thinks.

Or the husband spouts out, *I wasn't really talking to anybody, Jeff and I were just sharing our frustrations as we were working on the roof.*

Okay, I may be a bit sarcastic in that thinking, but I am around a lot of people and I know I'm not far off in how many people react to a problem.

Sometimes we talk more about what happened and get everyone else's opinion about what we should do, more than talking to our spouses about the problem, trying to find the resolution. We share deep, intimate details about last night's fiasco with a friend or family member who joins forces in our frustration, which only creates more havoc down the road.

If we agree that God is Wisdom, then why is it so hard to discipline ourselves to run to Papa if He has all of the answers anyway? I don't think we have accepted and truly understand that He does. If we have a hard time hearing Him, we just give up because we want the answer now instead of pressing through until we hear! He listens, He speaks, He comforts, and He heals, but we have to sit still to hear it, to embrace it. It is a discipline to quiet all of those voices in our heads and listen with our spirits.

Usually my initial reaction as I was crying out to God was, *Would you do something, make him straighten out and fly right!* I was focusing my cry in the right direction—but with the wrong heart, the wrong motive. What starts out to be what seems like childish tattling slowly grows into maturity, which is conversing with Perfect Wisdom!

What we do at the point of extreme conflict reflects the level of maturity in us. But everything is a process, isn't it? Every time I would get upset, I would go running to Papa telling Him what my husband did or is doing to hurt me or our relationship. I disciplined myself to *not* go running in any other direction, but straight to Papa, slowly realizing that was only the first step.

The next step had to be to check my motives in what I was saying, why I was saying it, and what I was really asking. Conviction would grow quickly in my heart motives and He would address how I was speaking about my husband. It is seriously amazing to be in extreme anger and try to talk to the purist form of Love Himself, and find myself not wanting to get angrier, but being brought to Peace as I would press into Him for the answers.

Papa would always—every time, and I mean every time—point to something in my heart in that moment; something that He wanted me to choose to walk in Love (in Him). I may not hear Him speak it instantaneously, but sure enough, it always comes faithfully. I believe He spoke it initially, but I could not always hear Him because my anger, pain, and frustration were too much in the forefront.

As I chose to forgive and release the pain and frustration, and believe the best of my husband and of our marriage, I began to hear what God was speaking to my heart of what He desired to see rise in me.

At first, when all that I heard from God in these moments was how I was encouraged to change, I was upset because it seemed as though God wasn't dealing with my husband; but I chose to let go of all of that and do what God pointed at in me, adapting myself to become Love. I chose to believe that God was responsible for my husband. I gave my husband to God and let go of trying to make anything happen. I chose to just believe for every place of breakthrough for him. I say all of this in a moment—but actually this releasing, letting go, and trusting God took constant effort on my part!

My focus became working on maturing my heart in Love, focusing on God rather than what the problem was, or seems to be, in the moment.

It has taken years of running to God to find breakthrough. Going to God is the safest place to share intimate details. He responds to what is best for me as I trust Him with everything else. He doesn't give me any negative opinions about my spouse, as some people might. He doesn't hold onto any negative thoughts if I was angry and was negative when I initially shared my heart, not realizing it myself, and He always has wisdom that paves the way through every issue for me.

It takes daily effort to hear Him, allowing the Word to come alive in you, to know what His heart thinks about things and people. It takes discipline to practice living in the spirit to see the vision. If you are convinced He is the best Person to run to, then there would be less resistance in being still to hear Him. If you are convinced He wants greatness in your life more than you do, and you know if you are left to your own you will either make a mess of things or you will not succeed to the fullest; then it's easier to run to Him for the answers.

I do not believe there is a need to seek any other opinion if you haven't asked God's first. If people's opinions rank higher than God's, I believe this is a very dangerous place to walk. I know this firsthand. I cannot say I am completely free of caring what people think, though I am not who I used to be and I keep progressively trying to make God my refuge in all things. It's dangerous to be bound by caring what people think, but also I believe it's just as much so to not need others, or God's opinion, and only rely on yourself; this leads to pride, which is a whole other arena.

If we have a habit of running to others, we need to check our motives. Some people say they just need to "vent." I just want to ask, if that venting brings another down, what is really the purpose of the quest? Honestly, I haven't met anyone greater to vent to than Papa. He is always committed to my spouse's and my best interest. I get the results that I need in my own heart more quickly from Him.

If God says to seek wise counsel, then He will orchestrate our path and relationships in doing so. He loves to move through His people in helping each other, yet it cannot take precedence over are relationship with Him.

My husband and I have sought counsel at several different stages during our marriage, but there have been many, many more stages when I took it only to Papa and received wisdom and healing through Him, supernaturally. There is a consistent progression: pray, see results, heal, pray, see resolve, even if it may have been but a fragment in the moment. Sometimes it was just enough to keep believing and keep focused on the goal.

Authentic Love has Pure Motives

I believe it is healthy to question our motives behind all of our actions, but especially question our need to give our opinions to each other. If the end resolve is to expose or momentarily to just release anger and frustrations, I believe it will not give us the fulfillment for which we are longing.

My mom has always taught us: if you don't have anything nice to say, keep your mouth shut! She didn't just say it, she modeled it for us. For this, I am truly blessed. This admonition has put a strong desire in me to not get pulled into the "air your dirty laundry" mode that only tears people down.

I don't feel it is ever honoring or right to talk about anyone negatively to another. I diligently work on not even allowing those thoughts to surface; if they do, I quickly surrender them.

If you don't want your spouse or others to talk negatively about you, don't sow that kind of seed or you will reap that kind of harvest. If you need wise counsel, there are ways to share to get wisdom without being negative, putting the other spouse down, being judgmental, or critical. **I believe if you cannot figure out how to talk about it in the right heart, then it is not time to shar**e. Timing is everything.

In a business environment, if there were problems with the way things were being done, I would tell my employees, *I'm glad to hear about it as long as you can present to me a solution.*

If we see a problem with an individual or protocol, then I believe we should see some form or fragment of solution, if we spend time thinking about a resolution. Sometimes it may be we who need to adapt to the situation until we see the solution. My goal was to create a team. In a team we take on a different attitude. Situations are not one-sided—one person is not controlling in a team.

I would always listen wholeheartedly to see if changes were beneficial. There are usually situations to work out and improve, but if complaining until there is change is the motive (which can be control and manipulation), it doesn't build the business or relationships.

We can't complain unless we have insight to a change. Sharing an observation about something that is not working is desired—not complaining. Being insightful takes thought and self-analysis in motive, especially if the goal is to build wholeness. If employees can take on the heart of the team and know how important their roles are in the big picture for the business they start to care about the whole.

If there are legitimate problems, God will teach and show resolve; but sometimes it comes through a lot of seeking Him for the answer. He is more concerned about our hearts communicating effectively in Love than giving resolve, which is simple for Him.

Please hear what I am saying. I am not saying that my employees could not tell me when there were issues. What I *am* saying is that laying a ground work of team effort by knowing and understanding motives is critical in how we communicate problems to one another. Having this ground work establishes a trust in the resolve from both ends because our motive is unity.

Yes, I did have employees get frustrated with my response at times, but then we went straight to the motive of the heart. When we know we are unique, important, and have a voice, we start to thrive in all areas of our life. We do not have a deep desire to control and manipulate, but start to trust God in the whole picture.

I believe if we are not willing to be part of the changes necessary for success *(and a lot of changes require positive outlooks for success)* in business…it may be a wrong fit; in marriage it's lack of commitment.

Authentic Love is real, so we can spare a lot of heartache and pain in the midst of life and bring encouragement to each other, if we are willing to be transparent with our lives and share with each other what is working and what is not.

I don't share instances of my life because I pride myself in them. I share because this is what God has taught me and it has proven effective and with good results. I believe God has and gives everyone something to give and something to get! This is the oneness for we are created for.

⌁⧓⧓⌁

Don't touch My anointed, was God's response to David, when David was going to overtake him. Both David and Saul were anointed by the Lord; and though Saul had tried to kill David several times prior, God's heart toward Saul was still, *Don't touch My anointed,* and so, He allowed him to live.[42] What would change if we would grow in that kind of honor and respect for each other, despite our idiosyncrasies? God's heart *is* saying about His creation, *Don't touch My anointed*!

Though we as husbands and wives are not fighting to the point of wanting to kill each other, well let's hope not, what if we used that perception to cause a healthy boundary to arise between us—a respect and honor that we don't want to talk negatively or put each other down.

What if you perceive your spouse as God saying to you, *Don't touch My anointed* as *Don't speak or think negatively toward your spouse because he or she is My Treasured Possession?*[43] It is great affirmation knowing that God is speaking the same to your spouse about you. Believe that God is vindicating us to each other.

Realistically, I understand we are flesh and it gets intense between couples at times, but I have made this my goal, therefore I try very hard to walk in it daily. It is very challenging in the midst of conflict, but extremely rewarding!

God has taken me from a foul-mouthed, loose-lipped, angry person, and He is giving me His heart and He has purified my speech. He is teaching me His perceptions that are continually evolving in me; so, I am sharing all of this with you because I do not believe there are any excuses of why we can not live in fullness. I am thoroughly convinced, If God can transform me from the pit as He has done—He can do it for anyone!

AUTHENTIC LOVE CONFRONTS

One of the biggest problems in many relationships is the lack of confrontation in Love. Our battle is not flesh and blood. It is a spiritual battle. This battle requires believing, praying, taking authority to dismiss the enemy in the situation, and standing in it until all is fulfilled. I believe our part with flesh is to communicate in Love and communicate well. Being transformed into Love is the warfare! Confronting in Love is necessary for our own personal growth, but also to help draw healthy boundaries for our mates so as to not allow hindering and unhealthy barricades in our relationships to stifle us.

Confrontation does not have to be negative. Many have not seen examples of healthy, loving confrontation, so we are fearful of it. I think we as a people assume a lot about each other, and I believe we are incorrect many times. When we assume negatively, most times, if not all of the time, we are wrong. We may be correct in what an individual is doing, but we often judge the motive of their hearts, which is not Love. We can be matured in discerning of spirits, yet still we may judge each other's motives and hearts through our own insecurities or life experiences and end up greatly inaccurate. I don't believe we purpose to; I think we just haven't pressed into the heart of Love in that area yet. Sometimes we need healed from past offenses to see more clearly into the heart that is in front of us.

If we are judging a person's motive, it means we are accusing them of the reasoning for their actions. We are called to believe the best about each other, no matter what the offense.

Every individual feels they are right in what they choose to do. They may feel conviction, but they also feel that they have the right to do what they do. I believe the truth is if they knew God and understood His ways, they wouldn't walk the same path. If they really knew Him, they would be moving more obviously in transformation.

If we assume the best and think positively about someone, even without proof, even if the other has initially meant harshness, we are walking in Love. Believing for the best sets us free in our spirits!

So how does that apply when you have shared with your spouse how you feel about your frustrations and disappointments, and your heart's desires remain unmet? Or maybe you haven't shared recently with them, thinking, *He should already know, right? I have told her twenty times or so it seems. My husband knows how I feel.* Assuming your spouse understands fully can be a mistake and may be the reason why he or she is still making decisions that bring adversity in your marriage, causing more pain, and destroying the relationship.

The Truth is if we believe the best of them in their hearts, which is Authentic Love, we stop the negative cycle. If we are walking in Love ourselves, even if our spouse is walking in blatant destruction, God will defend and move for us. It takes diligence, patience, and persistence to focus on God and not the spouse or the issues.

To lovingly continue to paint the picture of fullness of what you see for your marriage, and affirming your desire to meet their needs, to be all of what you were created for to them as a spouse and as a best friend, this opens the door to a healthy cycle of marriage and for Love to flow. I believe if your mate continually hears and sees your passion to be all that you were created be for them, it promotes a desire to do the same.

I believe God will give you your heart's desire if you delight in Him! The key is to be open to whatever that looks like. For example, it seems as if I have shared my heart with my husband over and over. I would get annoyed hearing myself say what I felt were the same things for twenty years. To my surprise after many conversations about repeating myself, my husband's response was, *Well I must need to hear it over and over till I get it.* He wants to get it. He is sorry I have to repeat myself, but some things just seem to take longer than others. So apparently, it is *my* heart that needs to change its perspective about judging what I think the conversation is and what is happening in it. I have to *believe* the best and *listen to his heart* to get into greater oneness.

Can you see from this instance, that what I thought the problem was, was *not* the problem that I was asked to focus on? The problem was not that I had to repeat myself and he couldn't hear me; the problem was the lack of my ability to listen to his heart. Though I had felt

I had said the same things over and over, apparently I was not relaying my heart appropriately to him. This is what God was speaking to me. The only thing I am called to change is myself and adapt to Love. If you do your part, you will begin to see God doing His!

Here again, I had to ask myself, *what is the motive of voicing my opinion?* If I had a mission to get my husband to agree with me by nagging and complaining to drive my opinion home, I doubt he would respond by wanting to evolve together. I believe it would drive him nuts. It would drive *me* nuts if he did that to me!

Recognizing our own motives and choosing not to judge others' motives, comes from a lot of soul searching and listening for God. It is exhausting at times, but fruitful! I am only required to take responsibility for myself. We all have different issues and have different places of healing needed.

If my position for this season is to communicate my heart to my husband better, then that is what my focus is, however long this season lasts. If it is focusing on intently listening better, then that is where my heart is.

A major key out of frustration and into freedom is
to be thankful for what you do have, instead of, frustrated
about what you don't have—trust God with the rest.

A frustration may be a spouse that is distracted with busyness, a hobby or an addiction. Focusing on any and all part of the goodness that comes from them being in your life has to come to the forefront of your thoughts to enter into thankfulness.

At this point, I encourage you to pause a moment and think about any frustrations you may have and purpose yourself to put them aside as you look for how you can be thankful about **everything else** around and in your marriage and your life. Do not stop until you get into that streamline of thankfulness. What you will quickly realize is that if you keep pressing into thankfulness long enough, those frustrations slowly start to shrink compared to all of the other goodness in your life. Recognizing Truth and adapting our hearts to Truth is life!

Purposely remind yourself that this frustration that seems impossible to be resolved, "I was created to see...(speak the frustration)... become possible!"

– 6 –

Accept and Adapt

MATURING into Love does depend on our ability to recognize, accept, and adapt to the Truth in life. None of us have it all together, and we all need each other to speak truth at times, as well as learn how to receive it, especially with our spouse. How we present it is crucial to the oneness we are after.

I am a person of realness—I mean what I say and I say what I mean. I cannot compliment someone about their sweater if I don't really like it. The downfall of this trait is when people ask me a question, the answer could hurt their feelings. I try to be sensitive to their hearts, in these times, but I am still real. Over the years, God has softened my approach and still works with me in this, to be sensitive to how each one may take what is shared. I am a pretty forward person so it is sometimes just so black and white. What I have learned is that people's hearts are usually the gray area between. Sometimes the truth does hurt, but personally I would rather walk through the pain for a time and be in truth, than to live in deception. Some would prefer not to deal with the reality if the only way to receive it is through pain.

I believe it is extremely important to be sensitive to how we share truth, recognizing, if we are not careful, we may cause undo added pain to the already complicated situation, or to a heart that is already wounded. The Truth does set us free, but it needs to be coupled in Love.

For instance, if my mentor had not told me the hard truth that I was singing off key when I was learning to sing, I would not have realized the need for voice lessons. Would I have seen the gift that God was bringing through me as His gift to the depth that I do, or would I think it was my efforts and skill? I probably would not, because it was very humbling to receive and accept this truth.

I believe the whole process was definitely for my benefit for two reasons. At a young age my dad tried and tried to teach me to sing. He had to surrender his efforts, for he thought I was truly tone deaf. Then for Dad to see what God did in my voice after I kept pressing in, it was a miracle to him because he witnessed it. The second great benefit was for me to understand that I, at trying my absolute best, was completely off and I didn't know it. This was a great understanding in itself—*even when doing our absolute best; we can still be totally off.*

And to throw, to you, a whole other wave of God's teaching to me, He gave me a vision of going to sing and worship over a woman as she was dying and crossing over into the heavens. He wanted to pour through her in this and teach me. I didn't know at the time that I sang off key, but I was obedient to His call. As I worshipped, the awesome presence of God moved on this woman; I was honored to be part of that experience. Her response was full of tears and she said, *That was the most beautiful thing I have ever heard.* She crossed over into the heavens a couple days later. Had I not obeyed I would have missed an extreme turning point in my life and an awesome teaching of God's heart.

It was two weeks or so after that, I realized, I sang off key. Why did God do that? I truly believe He was teaching me that He looked at my heart before He ever looked at my skill. Authentic Love can override all of our weaknesses! He was teaching me that He can make anything sound amazing! This experience has given me the courage to stand up in a large group and worship because I know that He cares more about my heart than how I sound. He is teaching me excellence so it is natural to desire to improve, but the greater Truth is that as long as my heart is postured in humility in Him, He is there with me.

If we want to accept truth we need to
acknowledge what we focus on!

What's Your Focus?

What we focus on is what we pull to the surface in each other. We either make room for negative or positive attributes.

I will tell you though, the more I focus on the greatness and the amazing parts of God moving in my husband, it seems the more those parts keep expanding, or the more I can see of them. Do you hear what I am saying? If we focus on the negative, the more negative we will find! On the contrary, the more greatness we focus on, in our spouses, the more greatness we will find.

I love and adore the strength in my husband. The more I affirm it in him, the more I keep seeing! I can honestly say that I could not see his strength before I had a mind shift. A *You mean everything is not about me?* shift. I decided to focus on what I was created for and be that. I decided to focus on what I can do to be a better wife, instead of focusing on what I want, even need—trusting God for all of that. Becoming Love requires a mind shift. It is a different focus and has a different purpose. I believe selfishness contradicts Love and it takes courage to recognize this Truth and then, accept it!

I love being amazed by new discoveries in my husband that were always there, but I just couldn't see them for my vision was blurry from pain, anger, disappointments, and frustrations! Could it be that as I was thinking in my heart so I was perceiving?

If we build up, encourage, and affirm to our mates what is Truth, it helps them to think, know, and become who they were always meant to be. I believe this helps align us for the fullness and oneness that takes us to ecstasy.

Purposely building up and helping others identify themselves with God's greatness is our calling to each other—especially our mates.

Warning to the wise: satan has *tried* to accuse me of not being honest because what I was speaking wasn't a reflection of obvious, apparent behaviors, yet~ no proof.

This is how the enemy tries to throw us off when we are aligning with God's will for our marriages. We need to see past each other's idiosyncrasies. This is how we make provision for the prophetic Word (the Word of God for our present and our future) in our lives.

So in speaking life to your spouse, it is not being dishonest or lying if you cannot see it happening all the time, yet. No, this is actually calling destiny to the surface in each other, focusing on Truth.

It is the same thing as if I am praying for someone and I get a vision of that person in scrubs. I share the vision with them and they share that they secretly had a dream of becoming a nurse, but never told anyone. They didn't know how the outcome would be or they didn't have faith that it could happen. Someone else affirming those visions in us changes everything! It gives us courage to believe.

We have to have our focus on Love to speak what is good and if we want to call destiny to the forefront in each other, we need to perceive it. When we focus God, we begin to see!

What you speak that is good, righteous, and building up, finds confirmation in people's spirits; and though they may not believe initially, it opens the door for them to become.

When you call destiny in your spouse to the forefront, it is affirming, speaking it to remind both of you of fullness and encouragement towards the goal.

We are to remind each other that Love is manifesting through and in us, to keep focused on becoming one in every place.

As a side note, when I decided to quit smoking (I smoked a pack and a half a day), I started exercising these concepts of calling things that aren't, as though they are, or should be. This meant accepting the Truth that God had broken every stronghold, and then, trying to adapt my thinking and my actions to that Truth!

God had brought me out of cocaine addiction, supernaturally, after overdosing and feeling like I was having a near-death experience, but nicotine was more of a struggle…strange, but true. Sometimes, He supernaturally delivers, and other times, we have to walk it out!

After I had tried to quit smoking many, many times and failed, I chose to believe God's Word; I made it my focus. Every time I would light up a cigarette, I would speak out, *I am not addicted, I don't smoke.* I kid you not, faithfully I kept praying. I kept believing. I kept speaking it. Those around me, especially others who smoked and tried quitting several times, as well, would say, *You are ridiculous*, and laughed as I continued to speak it and smoke. But honestly, you can't care what others think; what matters most is what God thinks and knows. If getting free looks like ridiculousness to some, I guess I am as David said, *Willing to get even more undignified than this* to live in freedom!

Faith is more powerful than addiction. I truly love it when God delivers me quickly, but sometimes it is the best for me to walk it out! I went through nicotine withdrawal, but the empowerment and tenacity that He put into my spirit, pressed me through! More than fifteen years later, I am still experiencing the blessing of Him delivering me from nicotine addiction. He didn't just deliver me, He set me in extreme motion to believe intensely. The attitude of "believing for greater" set me in motion for believing greater for my marriage and for all entities of life. God is *always* doing more than one thing at a time.

Some may have a hard time perceiving what I mean by speaking what you see God calling your spouse into. If you think and meditate on some obvious areas of healing that your mate may need right now, focus on them being totally healed. What does it look like? Patience, gentleness, a really great listener, a great communicator, sensitivity to your heart, and trustworthiness; there are so many areas that God would like to heal in all of us! Some attributes come quickly through just asking God to open them up for us. Others come through years of praying and believing, even modeling them for our mate, but are they still not God's heart manifested in us?

Accepting and adapting to Truth may look like this: when you raise your voice or use a harsh tone when talking to your mate, quickly take responsibility for it and apologize, and try to do better next time. You *can* stop it from happening; make it a desire to *not* want to act this way. Sin is always conceived in the thoughts, first, so keep pressing to suppress and surrender those thoughts to God till they stop coming.

If you have a lot of hardness because of pain right now, I challenge you to seek forgiveness in every place of pain. If you want to start a cycle of Love, for the next couple of weeks, only allow yourself to focus on what your mate has done that has been good, the things that your spouse may do that you love. At first, it may be hard to think such things if your heart is heavy, but if you purpose yourself to give God all your disappointments and frustrations and discipline yourself to fast negative thoughts, (do everything in your being to not allow the negative thoughts) and focus on the positive, *God will stream light into the darkness because He is Light. He is everywhere, even in the darkness. He is in the pain with you*[44] If you choose to let go and let God take care of each detail, you will trade up your quality of life. Believing the best is one of the greatest qualities of Love there is! It is true freedom.

See Frustrations as a New Vision

What if...seriously what if, in every frustration, there is a place where God wants to inject a new vision? Would you be encouraged to look for that new vision and let the anger disperse and flow into expectation of something new that God wants to move in you or in the situation?

I believe this is Truth! I have experienced this time and time again to the point where I try to go from frustration to looking for the new vision more quickly, viewing frustration as an opportunity to see a new vision.

I have been in pain and frustration many times and God is always faithful in bringing the light! Sometimes it takes longer because it takes me longer to fast the hurtful, painful, even angry thoughts *(surrendering them in forgiveness unto the Lord, not allowing them to linger in negativity),* trusting them all to God, asking Him to take care of each piece, even when I could not connect with a resolve. I see now as the Lord keeps healing my mindsets that the issues I thought were in response to my husband's choices, were actually caused by the lack of understanding and proper communication between us; not truly hearing what each of us were trying to say to the other, and not choosing to love each other properly.

Sometimes when my husband would get angry or frustrated at what was happening in the moment, I would assume he was angry at me. But now I see that his frustration was because he wanted to provide or love me a certain way and he didn't know how to get from point A to Z. I didn't, or couldn't see it. And because I thought he was angry at me, I would get irritated at his anger. Wow—what a negative cycle! If I had just believed the best intent of his heart, I may not have lingered in frustration as long. We are both learning to love greater!

I asked my husband the other day, *Are you pursuing me?* thinking I am opening his perspective to see his intent, yet also affirming my desire to be pursued. We all want to know we are pursued, right? I was the one whose eyes were opened to another level of understanding Love in my husband when he says, *I was pursuing you went I went out and risked my life in that hurricane to bring a generator back. I was pursuing you when I was sucking out the excess water in the sump pump when it was about to overflow and ruin all of your salon equipment.* I was the one whose perspective was opened, amazed at his response.

I am sharing this with ladies to hopefully expand Love in your vision as coming through more than words and emotions from your husband. I am sharing this with men to help encourage you that as women, we are tied so strongly to emotions, we don't always see the fullness in Love coming through all of your actions. There is always such room to constantly grow and mature. This keeps us humble.

I want to see and experience every part of Love! If we can just focus on what is happening that is good, this alone will cause us to worship and live at a higher level, causing us to lift our heads.

I cannot say it enough, press through the hard, painful places purposely into Love. Don't give up or run away. Keep believing the best is yet to come in your life, because it is!

If you are in an abusive marriage, walk with God through each step. I do not believe for a moment God wants any of His children to be in abusive relationships, but I also believe God can heal anything and anyone. Sometimes we have enabled the abuse, so when you have been entangled for years you have to walk out your part of Love, which I believe is first to accept the truth and then to stop the enabling. Follow God through each step, no matter how difficult. He will lead you to fullness and freedom. It is not about the easiest pathway. It is about the best pathway.

This is my best visionary for things that I have wholeheartedly tried to work through, taken responsibility for, and am actively working through in my own heart, doing my part, but sometimes I cannot fix the issue myself. I accept the truth that I can only change myself and obey what God speaks to me.

I throw it all up to God (surrender every piece to Him) and ask Him to give it back all figured out because I can't do it in and of myself! I choose to fast negative thoughts about it. I work on my heart, as I wait for revelation, trusting God. God is always faithful. Why fast negative thoughts? Because it *is* easier to think negatively when you are hurt or angry.

The key is to be faithful with what God points to in our hearts, as He shows you the new vision. There are ways that seem right to a person, but lead to destruction[45] so we cannot trust our hearts themselves, but the spirit within as we are humble to listen.

I have spent time praying a lot for my husband, and God is giving me His heart for Him. I started seeing from a whole new perspective. Then I started to agree with what my spirit knew, adapting to Love. There is always potential. We need to open it for each other.

As we open up insight for each other, it is most productive to test our hearts in how we can adapt to Love ourselves.

One of the greatest things that has sustained me in this process through the years is when one of my mentors said to me, *If you're praying for someone and it seems like there is a paper bag over his or her head, God probably wants something in **you** to change.* Funny, but very real and true! This has helped me tremendously to evolve and progress at becoming more loving.

Sometimes my husband and I have had no proof of making it through, just faith; an inkling of we are going to get through this. Sometimes only one of us had it at the moment, but it is enough if you stand together in it.

If you are walking with God, you are walking with Wisdom. He requires that you have faith, believing, and walk in Wisdom(Him)! He promises if you ask for it, He will pour it out without reproach. I don't think there is a day that goes by that I don't ask for Wisdom for situations. He is faithful to those who humble themselves to ask.

We need to use Wisdom if we step into encouragement by asking counsel, let it be just that~ encouragement for both of you. If we care about others not having a negative opinion about our mate, out of respect, then Love is moving. On the other hand, if you don't share for fear of what people may think, that is another issue—bondage.

Some may say, *Well I'm just speaking the truth about what happened.* I am suggesting that they look deeper to test their motives, looking to how they can adapt to Love and care about how things will come across.

When I started running to Papa about my husband, I could feel His heart sadden by my motives, but He kept embracing me and gently teaching me. He caused me to become aware of my anger and even my vengefulness. I learned righteousness in running to God with my issues. Now I run to get the answers to know how He wants me to adapt to Him.

Warning: If your motivation in running to tell God your problem is so He will fix it without any change or cost to you, you will be highly disappointed. He died so we may live as He is, pure and blameless.

We are being transformed from glory to glory. Not because we have to, but we choose to run to God because He has set us free and came to give us life abundantly!

If you are not living life abundantly, keep pressing until you are! He is setting us free in our mindsets continually.

I have come to understand that He desires us to choose Him, but He will not choose for us. If you choose Love, choose His ways which are higher and greater, then, your life will begin to soar. *Love, peace, and joy will start to abound and once you taste that, you will not want to relinquish it, but allow His glory to transform you progressively, purposefully. There is nothing greater!*

Experiencing God is radically life changing. So when I run to tell Him what is going on, not because He doesn't know, because He knows everything. He loves it when I take the time to talk to Him; and as I do, I am able to release pain in me, trading it for more of Him, Peace and Joy.

In adapting there comes a learning in how to just be: He shows me, my true self, compared to His Love and purity. He invites me to let go of attitudes and emotions that are not Him, and adjust my heart. He never forces me to choose Him. He desires it, but He does not ever push me.

When I go to Him, He shows me how to turn toward Him. What I think ought to be a conversation about my husband ends up being about me and my attitude, my heart.

Every time, and I mean every single time that I have been in a hard place in my marriage and I would be purposing to go find what new understanding I could get from His chapter of Love to help our situation, Papa would always point to something for me to work on personally. I was initially hoping to find something God would show me for my husband to work on, sad but true, just being honest. Then into maturity I was looking to see something for us both to work on, but He doesn't usually present it like that to me. It is usually just all about me, where and how He is calling me to be Love!

After many of these constant, reoccurring events (me running to God about my husband, God speaking to me about my heart, me confessing and changing and adapting to Love), I don't even have these lengthy discussions much anymore about what my husband is doing. I go straight to asking, *Show me how to pray for him and us, and what do I need work on in myself?* In this, peace comes, and I know my husband is in His hands because I released him there as I work on my heart—I cannot change my husband, nor is this my desire. I want my husband to be God's design, not my clone. I understand that I am not the Holy Spirit and I really could not do His job anyway.

And now, sometimes I can not honestly even make it past patience or kindness before conviction grips my heart and I confess, *You're right, God, I am not being patient to wait on You to move in my spouse,* or *God, please forgive me, I am not being kind.*

⊰〓◊◊〓⊱

My husband having his own thoughts and ways apart from mine is part of the romantic attraction. We may not perceive that, if we have control issues, but that is what creates the spark. Yes, if there are wrong motives moving, which causes adversity, it will lead to frustration, negating romance!

But if you keep lovingly reminding each other of the goal to become one, you start to see the greater picture, and selfishness and control start to dwindle, because God is moving in this marriage with you—if He is invited.

As I seek Papa's heart for whatever situation is in front of me, I wait for Him to teach and show me more of where He is calling me in Love. Without fail, I always receive a word from Him about something I am to work on. This leads me to believe that if my focus is stayed on me adapting and changing toward Love, then it will keep me from being in my husband's backyard telling him what he ought to be doing; I let God handle that.

You can be flat against the wall, angry, bent out of shape, confused, and frustrated, but if you release each emotion, each offense to God, you will begin to hear Him. One word from God can change your whole perspective, aligning yourself to hear Him and then choosing to believe it is Him. These are some of the hardest heights to achieve in yourself, but not impossible. The more you think it is Him and test it and see that it is Him, the more confident you will become in knowing that you are hearing Him because He *is* speaking to us!

If we are constantly working on our own issues, we won't have time or desire to judge or criticize others, because our passion is to become His heart!

Now don't get me wrong, my husband has to deal with what God points out to him. Some may say, *Well, my husband won't.* Please don't take offense at my reply in saying, that isn't your problem. It's God's problem, if you release it to Him. I say this with no attitude behind these words. Yes, I do understand you are one, together, and everything your mate does, affects you. I understand total frustration in this regard, but the best posture for you is to release it all and watch what happens!

Tell God all your concerns, fears, apprehensions—whatever, however it affects you. Then purpose to let go, let go of fear. Let go of anger and unforgiveness, moment to moment, daily. Let go of your mate in all unhealthy strongholds and expect God to move in the situation and in your hearts. I say hearts because if it concerns you, it is usually about you, too!

It's like the saying that if you point a finger at someone else, you have three pointing back at you is so real. Part of the reason you are unraveled is because it is reflecting a fragment in you that is the same as what is aggravating you, coming from the one to which you are pointing.

Honestly, I have found that to be so true that when I am pointing a finger, judging and criticizing, the truth is, something in that person that annoys me is the same thing I don't like in myself, or that I am trying to get free from. I believe that is a gateway to getting free of judging and criticizing others, but also to see what I need to work on in myself, if I'd adhere to its wisdom! Once I had realized truth like this I could let individuals be themselves and if anything arises I focus on asking God to help me get rid of it, praying for the other in the same way.

Your part in the marital relationship is to grow and mature in Love, and at times, it may only be to maintain Love in the waiting. From this point, wait on God to move. If you feel frustration stirring in you, dive deeper into the expression of Love. (Details of each entity are at the end of the next chapter.) This will help you focus on every area of your heart, test it and get the focus off your spouse. Again, if you have something in yourself to work on, it takes the focus off your mate and onto God. God will not disappoint you if your hope is in Him; not in Him doing what you want, but in Him moving, trusting the resolve is working for your good.

I believe God wants to prove His grace is sufficient for us! I believe He wants to prove to us that He is enough for us! It is when we hit hard places that we find out what we believe, and then we can choose to go deeper in Him, an awesome invitation that only brokenness can offer to us—or to tail-spin into selfishness, *I want what I want, my way.*

I am sharing what I do in instances, but I do not want to downplay how much I pray about the problem at that moment and every time any negative thought wants to persist. I have to surrender it again and again, however many times it takes. In really hard, painful places my worship, all day long— fifty times a day if need be is, *I choose to forgive.* I say worship because that's all I have had to give some days. I believe God is pleased.

He doesn't want only bits and pieces, or just the good stuff; He wants whatever we have to give. It is being in His presence that transforms and heals us.

I choose to believe God wants everything awesome to come in my marriage more than I do, but I know He is more concerned about my heart in the moment than fixing all my issues. I have learned if I am being Love, then all that is left is him (my husband) and Holy Spirit. In this, my husband is able to see more clearly where things need to improve, and he is free to take responsibility. If I am constantly nagging at him for this or that, then for him it would be easy to conclude that I am the problem. Do you see what I am saying?

Years ago after I read the Proverb comparing a nagging wife with a drippy faucet, I thought, *Ugh…I don't want my husband to ever think, feel, or perceive me as a drippy faucet.*[46] Nagging to me means asking more than once. This has been a plumb line I have drawn in my life. Does this mean I never repeat myself? No, it just helps me pay attention more to what I am saying. But it also helps my husband to listen when I am talking because he knows I don't want to repeat myself. It's a continual learning process intertwined with being sensitive to each other's feelings.

My motive is to better our marriage, not to establish my own plans. If we understand God's ways are higher, then we are more apt to pull back and discern before proceeding. If God directs and delights in our steps, He will establish them.[47] If we carry His heart for life, for people, for our relationships, He will affirm our way. He causes abundance and fulfillment in us to arise. Being humble and teachable is critical.

If someone would have told me years ago the answer to life's equations that would cause me to succeed, that would have helped me fulfill my calling and purpose in life at a whole new level, I hope I would have jumped in without hesitation. Right now I am committing to you this very thing, if you choose Love, it will fulfill, satisfy, and take you to a whole new level in life and intimacy in your marriage! Seems simple? Heard it before? Does your life give testimony to it?

I am submitting to you, if you purpose every time you engage in any kind of disagreement in your marriage, if you invite God into the issue, asking for wisdom with the heart intent to obey, to focus on becoming Love, you will see miraculous changes and long-lasting results. You will find yourself becoming a person you didn't know you could become. You will find a greater, deeper love for your mate. You will find strength you haven't known before. God will teach you how to process anger, disappointments, and frustrations more quickly.

The changes are not because all the issues in your relationship get fixed immediately, but because you are gaining a right perspective of their purpose in your life. You will see that these emotions take up space where peace and joy want to reside. The more you focus on God, the more you want to become like Him, and the more you want His desires and heart to flow through you! You will move through impossibilities in your relationship and in yourself. You will experience God! You will experience ecstasy!

Thank You, Papa, for leading me to recognize, accept, and adapt to Truth, to You. Thank You for teaching me who You really are—true, Authentic Love. Help me see where I am hindering You from having Your way in me and in my marriage. Help me to see the difference between my agenda and Yours. Cause my heart to be motivated by what motivates Yours! Help me to fully acknowledge when You convict my heart if I try to run to anyone else, but You, to vent or air my opinion. If You want to use godly counsel to help insert wisdom, point us to that person and open our hearts to hear it and walk in it! Show me how to live in ecstasy with You, personally and take us as a couple to higher ground where ecstasy resides all of the time and not in fragments!

Our marriage is a true gift from You. Help us to not take it for granted! Help us speak only words of life and encouragement to each other. Point them out in the midst of conflict, where it is hardest to see. Help us to speak Truth and not just echo facts that frustrate our goal of oneness. In every frustration, show us the new vision you want to bring forth!

No matter how hard things may get, let us know in our hearts and believe that You cause our feet to walk forward and make spiritual progress through every high place of trouble, suffering, and responsibility. Thank You for what You are going to do. Everything we are asking You for is Your heart, so we can believe and not doubt, as we wait to see the fullness of it all!

— 7 —

Always More!

Love is endless; therefore, there is always going to be enough and there will always be more! If we pull apart the expressions and entities of Love found in First Corinthians 13:4-13 and use them for a self-analysis, we will always find something to work on and work toward, in ourselves, and within our relationships, until the Perfect(Christ) comes.

After all, wouldn't you want your spouse, after you accidentally back into the garage door, totally destroying it and inflicting several hundred dollars' worth of damage on the car, to walk in Love in that moment...or in the next several moments? Or how about when the story gets retold? Wouldn't it speak volumes if your mate would choose to be kind, patient, and self-controlled because you already feel badly enough?

You would benefit if your spouse would choose to be slow to anger, quick to listen, and quick to forgive. Or, how about if your husband by accident puts the wrong, special ordered, expensive oil in the truck and he comes to tell you? He already knows he wasted money in the already-tight budget and made the mistake, he just needs you to tell him it's all right and not make a big deal about it.

If you could experience God's grace coming through your mates because they chose to let God come through, is it then more appealing for you to choose to walk in it yourself? It takes just one to start a healthy wave and for the other to receive the benefit to experience true Love. Talking and communicating your desires to each other is crucial as you paint the picture, for each to see the goals more clearly.

What about the husband who comes home to report that he lost all of your investments on an idea that went south? An idea that you only submitted to because you didn't want to fight about it anymore, and you had surrendered it to God. He may expect to find an angry, raging battle, but you had chosen to be one when you submitted to his desire, trusting God for the outcome. Though you don't understand why or how it all works, God still moves in faith in you about it because of your posture of Love.

I believe that Love coming through us is opening doors and will continue to open doors no one can shut! How would our lives incredibly change if we had such a pursuit? If just one in the marriage chooses Love, the course of life will be set in motion differently and it will cause a cycle that melts hard hearts.

It is very challenging if it is only one of you purposely pursuing, but so worth it! I encourage you, no matter how much understanding you have had in this Word of Love, to let God take you deeper in what it looks like. If you can take time to meditate on what it is, what it is not, what the Word really means in your motivation, your judgments, your expectations, and in your actions, I believe you will gain a new layer of revelation!

I would love having it all now (wisdom, revelation, knowledge), but I have learned and continue to learn to not despise the journey! The journey makes us who we are! In the journey you find brokenness that causes you to be still before Him, it causes you to look for Him in new ways! It is through precept upon precept that we learn righteousness. Everything is a process! I accept that I don't know it all already! I purposely posture myself in being humble so I can grasp what God wants to pour out. I know, if I don't humble myself, I will miss what He is saying, what He is teaching in the moment; therefore, I prolong being able to embrace fullness in my life.

Test your heart, challenge yourself to grow! Being real is the first step in freedom! Love has many, many layers! View it like you have never heard any teachings about it before and ask yourself some probing questions. When you are in the midst of a struggle may be a great time to refer back to these questions to hear God speak to you in this as well.

Becoming Love is an Evolving

Love endures.[48] Love never runs out, never runs away, it never abandons, never gives up. *(Am I enduring long? Do I believe with all of my heart, without giving up, for however long it takes, that God is moving in my situation? Am I abandoning a vision because it's hard versus knowing the Lord is redirecting my course? Is the motive of my heart focused on me or us?)* We endure long because there is always more to gain. Laying something down out of obedience is not the same thing as abandoning a vision. The difference is the spirit that motivates us whether it is fear or wisdom. There are situations that God asks us to let go for our own good; living with a spouse that is physically abusive or who commits adultery, not desiring to get help or change. These spouses can get healing and the relationship can be restored but to think you need to endure abuse is not Love. Learning how to endure through tough times is everyone's quest. This is what makes us stronger as individuals and as couples, it is in the breaking through.

Love is patient. Love understands that waiting on God means we must need more strength for what is ahead. *(Am I patient to wait? Am I okay with not having control?)* Impatience is usually motivated by fear—fear of missing it, fear of not getting what I want or out of a desire to just simply control. I can wait as long as it takes for God to move. I am willing to wait because I know the best is always yet to come! How long does it take to be patient? As long as it takes.

Love is kind. Kindness does things for people, even those who are undeserving. *(Am I being kind or am I full of hatred, anger, and frustration that I cannot even be polite or civil? Am I still serving my spouse like I am called by Love to serve?)* Kindness does things for people just because it is the right thing to do. Kindness sees worth in individuals and honors that. Kindness loves to make a difference just by helping.

Love is never envious, never jealous. Where there is jealousy there is all kinds of roots of evil. Jealousy is a syndrome of a deeper issue. (*Am I taking responsibility for the full calling on my life—aligning myself—and being open to becoming every piece of Love? Do I compare or compete with others instead of being content and appreciate all who are around me? Am I jealous of my spouse or their relationships? Do I know that everyone is designed for a great purpose? Do I know my purpose? Do I know and understand that everyone has something to receive and something to give? Am I realizing that I am important and I am breathing because God desires greatness to come from my life that He put there?*) Love never needs to be jealous because it knows there is always enough and we are each uniquely made and have specific giftings and character. Love knows we are all made with purpose and belong to the bigger vision in God's tapestry. We all need each other to be who we were created to be.

Love is not boastful or haughty. Love is not prideful, which is focused on self. (*Am I letting go of insecurity, focusing on myself or what others think of me, grabbing hold of the greater vision? Am I walking in fear? Has there been a standard put up in my mindset that isn't God's that I find myself looking to others for approval? Am I trying to find others in a worse place to justify myself? Am I content being who I am called to be and resting in that, knowing I have God's approval? Am I feeling a need to defend myself or my actions, or do I believe Truth will justify me?*) Whether insecure—not thinking enough of self, or conceited—or thinking too much of ourselves, love does not focus on us. It focuses on building up others as it properly loves itself. Humility compares itself to God only and sees how much it needs to grow. Love doesn't have to defend itself. Love doesn't need to prove they are right.

Love is not rude, unmannerly, or act unbecomingly. Love is neither harsh in tone, nor rude and sarcastic (saying what we do not mean or desire to be true). It is not short and abrasive with speech, body language, or stature. It speaks to edify others. (*Am I choosing to speak or decree over my spouse and my marriage what I know is God's heart no matter how tough it gets? Am I choosing to fight every temptation of calling my spouse names and eliminate thinking degrading thoughts? Though some attributes that are manifesting may be perceived as proof, they may be what seems like fragments of truth, but they are not truth. Am I choosing to believe the best? Am I being cold, rude, or harsh in my tone as I am speaking* to them? Am I looking for the new vision in the frustration?) Love cares how it speaks. It cares if it offends people. Love is always looking to learn and grow. Love is inviting.

Love does not insist on its own rights or its own way. Love knows it doesn't have to have its own way because it is humble in the fact that it may not be seeing fully in the moment. It recognizes that no one is perfect and some things are not as they seem. Love is understanding and submissive. *(Am I trying to control the situations because I know my way is better? Am I trying to control because I am fearful of the outcome? What am I really afraid of? Am I resting in the fact that I have surrendered everything to God and continue to trust that He will make a way through the impossibilities? Am I being faithful to let go and be responsible for my actions? Do I think I am right and need to make sure they understand my viewpoint and agree with me? Am I am learning to trust that what I am seeing for our future is God and He will finish what He starts? Am I choosing to be more loving than I choose to be right?)* I understand that Papa cares more about my heart adapting to Love than giving me everything I want, but I do believe He wants to give me everything in my righteous desires. Sometimes everything is not best in the moment and yet sometimes everything comes in time. I do believe all things are permissible, but not all things are beneficial for me.[49]

Love is not self-seeking. Love is not selfish it knows that everyone is important. It focuses on encouraging others. Love knows that God is moving through others for their benefit. *(Am I using people, my mate, or situations to advance myself or get what I want? Am I using my spouse to secure my addictions? Am I using my ability in being a quick talker to take the focus off me and onto a negative in my spouse? Am I seeking to even appear right? Is my focus to be all that I was created to be for my spouse or to get everything I can get from them? Do I expect them to meet every need I have?)* Love doesn't use people to get what they want. Love honors and respects everyone. Love doesn't manipulate even when it is obvious that they are right in a situation. The Truth is that if you are speaking Wisdom they will want to listen.

Our joy truly comes with being close to the Father and not by getting what we may think we want. It comes from Him pouring out His heart into us. Love doesn't put wrong expectations or negatively enables their spouse.

Love is not touchy. Love is not moody. Love is consistent in relationships. *(Am I walking on eggshells because of my spouse's anger or fear? Or do I cause my spouse to tense as I speak or loudly give my opinion? Am I moody at times where I see others become uncomfortable and pull away? If I get angry does everyone around me know it because I can't hold it back?)*

Being sensitive to people and not causing anyone to feel as though they have to walk on eggshells because of how I may react to issues is love. Love doesn't allow another person's anger to manipulate them, which is fear. God is not calling us to be manipulated or controlled by anything or anyone. He calls us to submit out of love for one another. There is no Love in fear. Perfect Love drives out all fear.[50]

Our mates can release a spirit of power and control, even fear, abuse—it is up to us whether we come into agreement with it, submit to it, or pray and rise up in the Lord in righteousness. We need to also test our hearts that we are not releasing any of these spirits, as well.

Sometimes the Lord, all of a sudden, opens our eyes to the emotional or verbal abuse that has been there all along, and He calls us to stand in it, but not receive it anymore. If it is coming from us, stop and take responsibility for it and get the appropriate help if necessary.

We can move in healing without separating, working wholeheartedly together in it and attain healing. It takes a lot of prayer, patience, and believing, but the situation can be healed, changed. Sometimes in the case of abuse it can mean separating for a time of healing. Sometimes it depends on the depth, form of abuse and the hearts willing to change that creates the avenue for healing. Each spouse may have layers of intensities to walk out.

God wants to heal anything, everything, and anyone—but the Truth is that not all of us are asking for healing yet. So, sometimes the focus in really hard situations is more about praying and listening to Papa's wisdom, than it is to do something, initially. If there is physical abuse and life threatening situations we may need to respond more abruptly, but even so in this God will lead each step if you look for Him.

Love is not fretful. Love doesn't worry. It is not fearful or anxious. It trusts God! *(Am I worried? Am I feeling alone? Am I unsettled about our marriage, about my mate, our future? Do I spend more time trying to figure the resolve than I do surrendering the issue and waiting on God to show me the answer? Do I believe I can hear God and that He will tell me everything I need to know? Do I find my self rethinking over and over because I second-guess myself or even what is right? Am I continually thinking 'what if this or that' with a negative outcome?)* The truth is God has us in the palm of His hand. We have to trust Him to move away from fear. He will never leave us abandoned, helpless, or hopeless.[51] Fear is a lie with which we are coming into agreement with. Fear will paralyze us in our circumstances. The Truth is we will never be alone because God is always with us. If we practice believing Truth, Peace will abound in and around us. God has great plans for us, and we *will* succeed.

Love is not resentful. Love is not resentful. It does not allow buried anger, unforgiveness, or bitterness. Love does not make provisions for vengeance, wanting others to pay for the hurt. Vengeance likes the feeling of holding the grudge because it's a form of control. *(Am I being resentful? Am I releasing every heartache, pain, and frustration? Do I want revenge? Can I look at or think about my mate without that irk in my spirit? Am I willing to pray and ask God to pour overflow into them till that irk leaves and is forgiven and released? Am I willing to try the same scenario again believing for greatness? Am I coming, giving all of myself, in this marriage again after having been through a shipwreck of pain?)* The truth is God loves to vindicate you, but it is His way, in His timing. Bitterness will always steal from you. Staying in an offense is a choice. Forgiveness is a choice. The desire and the emotions will follow after you choose to forgive. It is the one thing God commands and it is the greatest key to joy, ecstasy and peace.

To really manifest Love in situations of deepest betrayal is to pray for our spouses to the point that we know "What goes comes around comes around." We know and understand they will reap what they have sown. Bur our hearts want them so badly to know God and know conviction, that they would, themselves desire to break every stronghold, with God in their lives, and experience healing the whole way around. His desire is that we would love them so much that we don't want to see them suffer with pain, yet want to see them completely broken in the Father and choose righteousness, then be healed.

Love takes no account of the evil done to it. Love pays no attention to a suffered wrong. It doesn't allow others to abuse, it does not become a door-mat or stay in abusive situations; yet it plots no revenge. Love's only desire is to speak goodness. Love knows that Papa sees everything, and He defends the righteous and will one day make all things right. Love desires everyone to be healed. It does not bring up past occurrences in forms of retaliations to build greater arguments. It knows that Love covers a multitude of issues and Christ's blood is enough to cover all things. *(Am I rehashing things of the past in my conversations with my spouse out of a motive to pin him or her down? Am I being a doormat? Am I being pushy with my anger? Am I expecting my spouse to stand position while I talk down and degrade him or her? Am I quick to forgive because I truly release it to God, or because I am fearful my mate won't stick around? Am I giving my mate a clean slate in my mind every day?)*If we are moti-vated by fear, it isn't going to lead us to peace and it will probably try to control something or someone along the way thinking it is a form of pro-tection. We must work through each hurt and surrender it to get healing. Press through till the thoughts of revenge surrender. Each spouse receiving and aligning for healing is critical as a couple to move forward.

If your mate is not open to pray or even believe, then you pray and believe that your spouse will be open and be healed, and then God will direct the steps. So know and understand it may look different in your walk, but the end result is progressive healing.

Love does not rejoice at injustice or unrighteousness, but rejoices when right and truth prevail. Love doesn't celebrate when others pay for their consequences. It doesn't camp out and wait for others to pay. Love sees that we all fall short. Love understands grace. *(Am I looking for my mate to fall on his or her face from mistakes? Am I hoping to see the pain in my spouse's eyes… to hurt like I do? Because I know it is wrong what my spouse is doing, am I just* *waiting for the day of justice, hoping God will deliver vengeance?)* We all need His grace. Love doesn't see one sin greater than another. Love doesn't have higher expectations for others, even leaders than themselves in purity and in life. Love celebrates when they see God moving and doing great exploits through His people, supernatural, signs, and miracles.

Love, after forgiveness, lavishes goodness in every place. We feel raw in our spirits when we are wounded, then as we press into forgiveness with perseverance, all of that releases; yet God calls us to step up higher. We then pray for them to be blessed and truly know who He is intimately, and that He is in Love with them. If we have been deeply wounded, many times the healing comes in layers. As we choose to lay each wound down and forgive with all we are, we may feel completely healed; but as time goes by, thoughts are triggered through other circumstances, then again, we have to choose as was in the beginning to forgive with all of our hearts until it is fully complete. Be relentless in forgiveness! *(Am I willing to put Love and forgiveness before my wounded feelings or pride? Am I believing for double of everything that has been stolen from me and my spouse? Am I believing for the greatest in my spouse's life even though they keep wounding me in their selfishness and pride?)* Love believes when there isn't any proof. When things are erupting at its worst, Love still keeps believing.

Love bears up under anything and everything that comes. Love can believe all things are possible. Love is ready in all seasons. *(Am I willing to support my spouse's decisions though I have shared my heart and he or she is not doing what I think is right? Do I support my mate wholeheartedly, as one?* Wisdom—as long as it is not morally wrong. *If my spouse falls on his or her face, will I rejoice? Rub it in? Remind them in years to come about the failure? Will I lose confidence because I didn't have control, or do I truly believe that my mate is doing what is right? Am I committed to the point of supporting my spouse through extreme places where we do not agree, trusting God for the outcome?)* If we are aligned in Papa and moving with Him in all things, there is a trust that arises in us that causes us to be immovable, therefore we are looking for how and where we are to join Him. Love is focused on the whole moving and progressing, not just part.

Love is ever-ready to believe the best of every person. Love doesn't have a preconceived idea in a negative mindset. It doesn't judge or criticize. It discerns and prays, believing for outrageous goodness to pour out. Love walks in to a room full of people excited to see God's uniqueness in His creation. Love sees each individual as a gift from whom they can learn, grow, and exchange, but also see in themselves that they have something tangible to give. *(Am I believing the best in my spouse's motives of the choices they make? Do I believe the best even though I am walking down what seems like the same pathway in my marriage, hoping for the best, believing God is moving? Do I believe my spouse is trying with all of their heart to love me the way I desire?)* Love sees in the spirit. It sees past the hardness of heart. Love sees past annoying idiosyncrasies and looks deeper into the creative mind that is there. Love reflects God's heart to their spouse.

Love's hopes are fadeless in all circumstances. Love always sees or perceives hope in all places of life. Love knows there is always a way because God always makes a way. *Hope deferred makes the heart sick, but when desires are fulfilled, it is a tree of life. (No matter what the situation in our marriage do I believe there is always going to be a way to make it work? And do I believe we will not just survive but we will thrive and it will be good? Am I working at believing with everything in me and all that I am? Even if my plans do not succeed at first, am I continually hopeful and believing that God is only going to bring something greater in fulfillment?)* Sometimes we have desires that in the core are righteous; but, in the vastness of our dreams are not the finest of Papa's heart. Better stated: We may have desires to be loved a certain way, and we may have a perception of what that will look like. The core of that desire is knowing, being, and experiencing Love. If we are open to the vision changing of what that looks like, because God always wants to give us more than what we are asking for, we are then positioned for Him to blow our minds, and He will. It probably will just look different from what we thought it would, because He is always doing a new thing![52]

Love endures everything—without weakening. Love knows there will never be a good place to totally lose it, flip out emotionally, or fall apart because God will part the waters when it is necessary. Love knows that every single thing in our lives is for our good and His glory, even if we can't see it or feel it in the moment. God still promises good! Love understands that what we feel is our weakness, His strength is made perfect; therefore, we become stronger through Him.[53] *(Am I acknowledging God is moving through me in my weaknesses? Am I reminding myself at certain places that I am going to fall apart or totally lose my mind if such and such doesn't happen or if such and such does happen, which is only decreeing destruction? Am I agreeing with God that I can do all things through Him?)* The truth is our whole lives and everything we have worked for could be looking like it is all falling apart, but there is never a good time to lose it or fall apart emotionally. To think or to speak negatively, agreeing with destruction, will not lead to success. God's promises always hold true no matter what the difficulty. It is what we focus on that either sustains us in peace or enwraps us with fear.

Love never fails—it never fades out or becomes obsolete or comes to an end. Love understands that giftings, prophecy, interpretations, knowledge, all of these blessings from God will one day be superseded by Truth—but Love still remains. Love understands there is fullness and oneness coming! *(If any part of my heart or dreams I have had, died because of years of frustration and emptiness, am I commanding them through Christ to be resurrected? Am I keeping myself before the Father to live in this endless river of Love?)* No matter what happens in life, if our mates have been unfaithful or though our loved ones may have crossed over into the heavens, God never desires nor intends for any part of our hearts to die. We can mourn either situation, but the key is to release it. We need to keep ourselves sensitive to what we feel and believe. *(Am I vibrant in believing and living? Do I see, know, and feel my purpose in this life? Do I live this life with the intent of leaving a legacy of greatness, understanding if I am living there is great purpose to yet be fulfilled?)*

Faith is the conviction and belief respecting humankind's relation to God and divine things.[54] Faith is believing without seeing, not having proof. We cannot please God without it![55] Faith not accompanied by action is dead, empty.[56] If we truly believe, we will move in life in ways that prove that we do! ***Hope*** is the joyful and confident expectation of eternal salvation. Without hope our hearts turn away and may become ill. ***Love*** is true affection for God and others, growing out of God's love for and in us! Love can and does cover a multitude of sins. No matter how ugly things get, His

Love covers it. *(Do I believe that God is enough and He covers everything? Am I living in hopefulness to see it?)* Faith, hope, and Love abide, but the greatest of these is Love; to know Him!

If we truly want to rise in becoming a better person, vibrating at a higher frequency, being all that we were created to be, we need to accept the Truth of where we are in the process and take responsibility and change. It is piece by piece!

> *God, I acknowledge Jesus could do nothing apart from You. How much more do I need Your help? I believe You are doing new things inside me to help me see You as You really are. If there is any complacency in me, break it off! I want to be vibrant with passion in this powerful Love, in You! I cannot give my mate what I do not have, so I am asking You to pour Your Authentic Love into me, greater and greater, in fresh and new ways. Cultivate my heart to carry Your heart of Love, as I was destined!*
>
> *When I come to You with things that need more of You, allow me to hear and see what You are pointing to, in my heart, and adapt myself to You! You are so good! You will not relent in a heart that is for You! Thank You for pouring the understanding and the manifestation of Your Spirit in ecstasy over me and my spouse! I will keep believing and contending for Your Glory! I have all that I could ever need in You!*

– 8 –

Seven Ways to Encourage Ecstasy

1. **L ive your life as if you are actively leaving a legacy with no regrets**. Purpose yourself, daily, to be the best spouse that your mate could ever desire. Live every moment as though it were your last. Disagreements won't last as long, or go into a downward spiral, if you ask yourself this question in the midst, *Am I okay if this is our last conversation or the last words spoken to each other? Did I embrace my spouse before we parted today?*

We don't know when it will be our time to cross over into the heavens, so don't let the sun go down on your anger.[57]

In understanding what God was saying in this, at first I would refuse to go to bed until all was resolved, which sometimes meant keeping my husband up until 5 o'clock in the morning, even if both of us had to go to work that day. I think it is important to do whatever it takes to work it out, to get rid of the anger. I believe God says not to let the sun go down because if you get used to going to bed with anger, you begin to accept the angry spirit as normal living and it steals your joy and peace. It is important to live in forgiveness, actively choosing it, all the time.

Be humble, realizing you cannot do anything apart from God.[58] Be thankful for all of your gifts, skills, everything that He has worked in you, and be thankful that He has given you the ability to do them, recognizing these Truths. Invite God to move daily—constantly—in your life. Acknowledge, recognize, and know Him in all your ways and He will direct and make your paths straight~alignment.[59]

Learn the true joy in submission! There is a joy that releases when we align and posture our hearts aright! We are called to honor, respect, and submit to one another, in Love, not being barbaric, domineering, or controlling.[60] We are called to submit to authority as though it were unto the Lord.[61] As we take that heart into marriage, wives are called to submit to our husbands as heads of the household, in Love, not begrudgingly, but joyfully. We are called to defer to and adapt ourselves to them and, depend on them.[62] And we, as husbands, are called to love our wives like Christ loves the church. He died for her.[63]

Husbands are to honor their wives as physically weaker, but realizing that they are joint heirs of grace, so their prayers may not be hindered.[64] There is answered prayer and great joy hidden in the right motive of the heart; a core secret to oneness.

2. Consistently care about your appearance and being desirable.
Give your mate something to get excited to come home to every day.

If we have courted our mates by making ourselves desirable and then after marriage we don't put much emphasis on it, is that fair to our mates? Many prepared for their wedding day, months, or years ahead. We spent lots of time and money making everything perfect. Many diet to fit into a certain size dress or tuxedo. Women usually adorn themselves with makeup, special hairstyles, and exotic perfume. We are saying to our mate at this moment, this is what you are getting. So I am asking you, are we still full of all of that passion trying to be that desirable to our mate? If not, is that false advertisement?

My intent is not to cause an offense, but to take a deep look at ourselves to get the best results. We cannot change what we do not acknowledge as Truth. Health issues can cause a shift and may create some hurtles, but caring about our appearance is more about the intent of the heart, believing and trying our best. Many times our health is displaying the lack of Love we have been walking in for ourselves.

If we are inviting God in every effort and trying with all our heart to love ourselves, God will meet us in those efforts and honor them. These efforts include building self-esteem, learning to truly love who we really are, taking time to exercise, eat right, dress in clothes that enhance our beauty, not provocative, but appealing to our mate, showering and brushing your teeth daily. If we are truly about being everything we are called to be, we will care about all of these areas. We have been entrusted with these bodies. Are we being faithful with them? None of us are perfect, but we are trying our best in excellence. If we fall down, we get back up and go forward. Eventually, the diligence and perseverance will pay off, because we are choosing Him, Life.

Where are your priorities? Here's a perspective that may help you see where your heart is. If you shower, comb your hair, splash on some perfume or after shave to go out in public, but you won't take the time to do that for your mate, do you have your priorities out of order? If you care more about impressing others, or about others seeing you disheveled, it will affect your ability to press into ecstasy? To consider how your mate feels is the greater quest! Shouldn't your spouse be the first to get the best of you? I am not talking about being legalistic, that you can't sit around in sweatpants once in awhile. And as a woman, it is right to allow your husband to see you without makeup at times so you are not hiding behind it. This is not about dos and don'ts. It is about loving yourself and loving, respecting, and honoring your spouse. It is the core intent of your heart that creates oneness and fullness in your marriage, and establishes living in ecstasy.

I knew a woman once who never, ever let her husband see her without makeup. She would put fresh makeup on after her shower at night, and set her alarm to get up before he would see her, and go apply fresh again. No kidding! I believe makeup is for enhancing, not for hiding behind.

If we acknowledge our insecurities and get healing, we can then rise above them. We need to get to the place where we truly enjoy who we are, as we work on the things we want to improve in our being. If we truly love who we are, we then can truly love our spouse properly. We will want to take a shower, and desire to look, smell, and feel our best. Our mates should have these first fruits, otherwise we are missing the greater in front of us!

Beware of the "excuse train." When we struggle with disciplines in our lives, whether with exercise, drinking water, running late, healthy diet, we need to be aware that it is easier to give or find excuses than it is to make the change and press into discipline. My opinion is that we are the Body of Christ walking with His resurrection power, so shouldn't we *look* like the Body of Christ walking with resurrection power?

I say this with desire, not from a heart that feels I have attained it all! I know the excuse train all too well, myself. I don't want to give excuses as to why I won't make time for exercise or read the Word, or spend time with God.

We can find an excuse for everything if we want, but we forfeit abundance in doing so!

3. Purpose to build up your mate privately and publicly. If you have had intense, hard times in your life and need to break through a lot of hardness of heart and unforgiveness because of pain, purpose yourself to not rest fully until you break through all of that hardness. Don't be content until you attain peace in all directions. It is very difficult when you feel like you keep having continual frustrations and hurt. You are called to build up and encourage and the only way you will be able to rise above it is for you to keep focusing on Jesus. Keep believing for greater; let God orchestrate what that looks like, and you will see Him move!

We may not get things the way we have specifically asked or hoped for, though I believe God always wants to give more than what we are asking for, and in this, it may take longer to align the fullness, but it will come to those who believe!

Trust that God works every detail for your good—no matter what! He's got you, if you trust and walk with Him.

This is a pivotal key that causes many to stumble. Sometimes we have it all planned out so well that there is no room for God to move miraculously, or spontaneously. God loves to surprise us and give us far greater than what we hope for, imagine, or dream.[65]

Pray for your mate and see him or her from Papa's perspective in what strengths and gifts are in them. Start there in honoring and building them up. Look for ways you feel God wants to heal, and speak that life into your spouse to help it come forth. Write texts, emails, and put notes in your mate's luggage and vehicle. Leave them around the house. Speak what you are thankful for, words of affirmation, and the prophetic vision in them. Show your spouse your Love of who and what he or she means to you. Be creative and spontaneous. Spontaneity builds relationship and romance. Plan surprise getaways with things to do together you may not usually do, and if you are on the receiving end, be grateful and enjoy the time even if the plans were not your desires. Appreciate the efforts. Continually verbalize how your mate's life affects yours. Be a place of encouragement for them in all ways.

Don't allow yourself to criticize, put your mate down, or speak derogatory names in private or public. If you have those thoughts, purpose to work at not allowing them to conceive in your mind, being sad to touch His anointed like that, instead, believing the best.

Who can become all they were meant to be if they are torn apart in the core of who they are? If negative thoughts continue to come at them in the atmosphere, how much more difficult is it for them to press through in Truth?

Sometimes we need to speak truth, confront in love, but there are many ways to speak it. If we lovingly, gently help our spouses to see truth, they will be more apt to respect and honor us for that, knowing they can trust us with their hearts. Think before we speak; ask ourselves, *Is it going to build up or tear down?*

4. Discuss and disagree with intent and purpose to listen to each other's hearts and grow together. In the midst of a discussion or disagreement, it is very healthy, after each one shares their hearts, for each to say, "This is what I'm hearing" and then repeat what you think you heard. Then ask, "Is this what you are saying?" It is amazing how much my husband and I still do not always understand what is really being said. This is a perfect way to weed out the excessive back-and-forth, unproductive diatribe that usually ends up hurting each other. Work at being one with each other even in the heat of the moment. Make it your goal to grow in your desires to choose Love for each other.

Disagree with the intent to see the actual core issue. Many times, probably most times, when we have disagreements, the thing that seems to be the big issue is not the real core issue. If we do not deal with the core issue, anger and frustration continues to increase. We can't walk in full peace when there are underlying irritations and aggravations that we are not able to process or forgive until we speak them out and share our hearts.

Consider this scenario: Usually the wife is quick to forgive, but after a while she starts to get annoyed and angry at her spouse's decisions. He chooses to spend extra time on hobbies away from the home. He is hanging out with his friends while she is at home doing housework and taking care of the children. When he is home, he watches television most of the time. He occasionally helps around the house, but she is irritated that he doesn't do more or spend enough time with the children. And to top it off, the finances never seem to stretch far enough, no matter how much she works. She is continually fighting to believe God is providing, yet she is stressed that they won't get all of the bills paid.

So when she sits her spouse down to pour out her heart, she lets him have it, citing all the minute details. His simple and direct translation of her frustration: *So you want me to work more, get another job?* He just wants to fix the issue, so he offers a concrete solution rather than wanting to discuss all of the issues she has presented.

She thinks the problems are all of the above, but when she takes the time to ask God to show her the core issue, she realizes that she doesn't feel loved, wanted, or important to him. Yes, she desires help around the house; and yes, the extra spending on hobbies is not helping the finances. These things all need to be addressed, but the core, for her is the emotional distance between them. Maybe he thinks he's not needed or desired because she is so busy with the household chores and children.

Now granted, that may be an extreme case, but not far from how intense married life can get. We need to talk about every detail that bothers us as it happens and share them in love, sharing our heart's desire of what we would prefer.

I strongly, encourage you to find the core problem underneath it all to resolve the issues more quickly. Sometimes I do not get the core issue until I am in the pouring-out-my-heart mode and hear God speak it, right then. So being sensitive in the moment to ask and listen to what Papa is speaking is extremely important! If you know the issue, you at least know how to pray, even when you can't see the solution right away. This is the journey.

Some get fed up and put out with having to repeat themselves, or constantly fighting for their spouses to keep their hearts focused on the goal as they have committed. We all have weaknesses and strengths. We need to draw from each other and not throw separation or divorce words around for control, causing fear, as if these were options.

We are either committed, or we're not. If we allow each other to throw that white flag up every time it gets too hard, where are we going to end up? If we don't allow that between us, then we can clearly commit to each issue and work at both ends to establish the goal, not allowing fear to manipulate between us. One may be working at changing the behavior as the other is working at forgiving, both continually believing the best. Embrace the journey!

So to disagree or discuss with a purpose and to progress more quickly towards solutions, ask these questions:

- What is the problem or problems? Then repeat to each other what you feel you are hearing, listening intently to hear each other's heart.
- What is the core issue? Ask God and share what you sense to see if you both can confirm. Again, share what both of you are sensing and hearing what you think the core issue is.

If you are having trouble finding the core issue, these questions may help.

- Are my personal needs being met?

- Do I feel loved by my mate?
- As a husband, do I feel honored and respected by my wife? Is she sensitive to my needs? Do I feel trusted?
- As a wife, do I feel taken care of with provision, strength, and emotionally connected with him? Do I feel supported?
- Are there healthy relationships between husband, wife, and children?

The goal is to admit and accept, so your relationship can move forward. Keep finding ways to explain until you both understand each other. Then you can progress and agree to work on the areas or talk about how you will try to work out the solution.

Sometimes we find fault with others because it is easier than blaming ourselves and taking the responsibility to change.

At times we may be drawing to the surface what we think are our mate's failures when it is really we who feel guilty for not having a good relationship with the children, or it is us choosing to work, over spending time with our spouse. We may be extremely overdue in receiving affection and we just may need a hug or conversation with our mate, to feel important—not that those things will fix every problem, but it is very true that if we try to meet each other's personal desires, it makes us stronger to deal with everything else. It keeps the irritation from going in all different angles from what the problem really is.

If you can't see what the issue is, ask God, He will tell you. It takes time to unravel when there are several different issues; be tenacious for unity and peace.

Sometimes all I need to hear my husband say is, *I'm trying my best.* When I know and realize that he is, though I may not see proof in the moment, I can rest in knowing that God will finish what He started!

Probably one of the boldest things my husband ever did when I was extremely angry and frustrated and pouring out my heart, was to hug me; and, he didn't just let go right away. I say it was bold because I was extremely angry, and to hug someone in that state takes courage! When his love began to penetrate the frustrations, I began to receive healing. It didn't solve the top issues, but it did help heal some of the core issue that I didn't realize I was in need of at the time.

This was such an awesome teaching to me about finding the core issues. We can have a lot of things going on, but if we are praying for each one, being faithful to what we see to do, talking and sharing our hearts continually, God is moving in the midst! If we keep being faithful and we will reap the rewards because God's got our back!

Most importantly, I am affirming in the midst of conflict, not to allow any room for regrets. So don't part with each other, for any reason where you would regret the last words, or heart, spoken to one another. We will live with our decisions and the consequences of them.

5. Study your mate, create, and maintain passion! Take the time and pay attention to the details of what your mate likes, loves, can and cannot handle. What makes him or her feel loved, their love language. What excites and frustrates your spouse? Weaknesses? Favorites? What fragrance does your mate enjoy on you? I believe women care just as much as men do about this.

When dating, we naturally pay attention to these things, but there is a greater connection when we see how these preferences change and acknowledge it to one another. This creates more passion, romance, and a deeper intimacy.

Find ways to speak and express that he or she is the only one for you, establish a deeper bond by affirming this often.

God leads us in all ways, if we are acknowledging Him.[65] Sometimes it is through discontent with things, to take us to a higher place.

For example, my husband's preference is for me to wear a bikini swimsuit. The more I continue to grow in the spirit I felt a greater pull toward modesty in my dress. I was torn between giving my husband what he desires and the conviction of teaching my girls modesty as they were growing up. As I continued to pray and seek wisdom, I felt led to ask my husband if he would go swimsuit shopping with me. I suggested that he pick what he wanted me to wear at home in our back yard or on the boat when others weren't around, and I would wear a more modest swimsuit in public. He was good with that. I believe this compromise created something more special between us because it gave him a greater sense of me being reserved for his eyes only.

Observing some differences in men versus women; they say men are more stimulated through visual and women more through intellectual, but I believe it depends on the individual.

Ask the questions, pay attention to the answers, and be creative in bringing new life to your relationship.

For example, I knew a couple who, before going on vacation together, weeks before, would intentionally come up with questions they had never asked each other before to stimulate conversations and invoke different insights and emotions. They purposed to not allow their relationship to get boring or mundane. If we want different results than status quo, we must purpose to do things differently.

Also, I believe every couple has a good sexual intimacy rhythm; time frames that work best for both. I believe it is very healthy to ask your mate continually, if he or she is satisfied through life, not take it for granted.

What do you feel is healthy in intimacy in respect to your mate's desire? Unity is important. It is always about ebb and flow, giving and receiving.

I have met couples that the husband demanded sex every day, and if it didn't happen, the wife would be treated rudely.

I think if we truly want the most romance, the most ecstasy, both spouses need to be equal parts of the equation. This is what marriage truly was meant for, to become one, not to bow to the other's addictions. Can we honestly say we love our spouses if we would treat them harshly, or with indifference because we don't get what we want?

From my experience, my husband and I have died to a lot of selfishness to bring forth the level of oneness we have now.

What do you want as an end result? No addiction or manipulation will give you true ecstasy. I encourage you not to use any kind of props and to seek only each other to fulfill the desires of intimacy. If you both agree to *only* be stimulated with and by each other, this will open up new places for creativity, passion, and romance.

I have heard of a godly man who counseled a couple, speaking to the husband with this thought, *If you treat a woman as she was created to be treated, loving her like Christ loved the church, you will never need to approach her for intimacy. She will approach you.* This is very true for me.

Some women who have been severely abused may need more encouragement and healing, but if you show her, she can trust you with her heart; deeper intimacy will come by faith as you walk through the principles of healing and love.

If you honor and respect your husband like he was created to be, honoring and respecting with your tone of voice and how you relate to him, I believe he will desire to approach you for intimacy. If you adapt yourself to him, truly coming alongside as his helpmate, appreciating the strength he brings, it creates a deeper level of trust in his heart—and yours.

I try to maintain an excited appeal, a righteous desiring of intimacy for my husband. I try to maintain the thoughts that keep butterflies in my stomach. I believe that the honeymoon never has to end. I believe it can only get better if there is commitment—and with God being in the strategy.

6. Be very purposeful about maintaining touch. Try to show affection as much as possible. Studies of healthy communication teach that it is beneficial to touch a loved one every time you pass them in the house. All humans thrive from interaction in touch. Every human needs and wants to know and feel loved and wanted. Making an effort to touch shows and communicates acceptance, Love. Studies have been done to prove the importance of touch and how newborn babies need to have it to thrive, otherwise they don't survive.

If we have not been hugged, loved, touched, told "I love you" as a child, a hardness can result as a way to protect ourselves from being rejected and hurt again; it also results because we have become desensitized to it. Touching may be awkward, but it can be broken through with diligence.

If one of you is more affectionate, draw on that strength until you become one in greater affection and touch. If you are shunned at times, believe the best and share your heart in how that affects you.

Most who are walking in shunning or a form of rejection do not realize they are pulling away. Most instances it is not intentional, in the heart of their hearts; subconsciously they may be protecting themselves from getting hurt again or they are just not used to it, needing healing.

7. Invite God into every place and take spiritual responsibility in praying for your mate daily. I understand I cannot do anything without God. It is because He puts His breath in me daily that I awake. I know He has called me into this life now for "such a time as this," just as He is calling you to live and have a radical, abundant life. There is only, and ever will be, one you. He put gifts in you and aligned your destiny alongside others in this life to weave an awesome tapestry of fullness and oneness.

So how can we try to walk this life out in radical awesomeness, staying right in step with Him?

The more I look for Him, the more I see Him. I share all of this to stir up a passion to seek Him, because honestly the best mate to be is one who allows and asks God to fill them daily.

If we walk in this posture, we always have something to give. We don't look to our spouses to meet every need, putting unrealistic expectations on them but allow Christ to fill us the way that is best in each moment.

Sometimes, fulfillment is through your spouse, and sometimes it comes supernaturally through God fulfilling that need.

Take time to pray for your mate, inviting God into healing every area and agreeing for God's heart in your lives. You will begin to see lasting fruit that causes you to continue with a hunger for more.

There have been many, many times, if not years' worth, where my prayers for my husband's heart to be healed translated into me seeing in the spirit, a glass pitcher of liquid gold pouring over him everywhere he went. Prayer isn't meant to be a task or a chore, but a relationship, simple love for the Father and receiving His Love; then He fills us, He opens our eyes to see, and teaches us how to truly Love.

God does not demand anything from us, but asks us to forgive as He has forgiven us. A life full of God's alignment (His blessing, His joy, His peace, His ecstasy) doesn't just fall on us; it doesn't just happen that we may take it for granted. He desires to be invited. He gives us all things, through Him, to succeed, but they are that, *through Him*.

I want to leave you with one of the greatest revelations of ecstasy I have come to understand. Because God has made intimacy, and created sexual desire in purity, and because we invite God into every part of our lives, doesn't it seem natural to invite God into our sexual intimacy, as well? I know this is a shock to some, but I encourage you to talk to God about it if you cannot embrace it now.

As I began to understand more ways of stepping into ecstasy with my husband, I very purposely and wholeheartedly invited God, Jesus, and the Holy Spirit into every part of the deepest places of intimacy. To intently embrace and experience God in the most sacred, intimate places of marriage, through worship. God showed up so unbelievably that He left me with no choice of ever wanting to be intimate without Him again. I guess you have to test it yourself to know!

This desire is from a heart that truly wants God, fully in all places. Though in the onset it may feel uncomfortable in thought ask yourself, *Does it seem like God's heart from the beginning of time?* Then ask God if this idea is of Him—*to have Him in every place in our lives.*

I heard a well-known speaker share, years ago, that she felt that praying in the spirit was foremost unto the Lord; and then into your marriage, for when you're ministering to your husband. When I first heard that, it hit my spirit like, the idea is so different, but it seems so right. As I continually conversed with God about it, I felt He affirmed in me that it was right. So, I have walked it out talking to God and my husband about it, because it seems logical in the sense that we were created in the Garden to live and have relationship with God all the time, not shut the door and see Him in an hour or two.

For many years I have prayed and continue to pray and invite God, Jesus, and the Holy Spirit into the bedroom. I pray for the anointing of love, the anointing of romance, the anointing of intimacy, and the anointing of God's ecstasy. I pray about everything that comes to mind as we come together, every time. But also I spend time praying ahead, if we are having a hard time getting together because of schedules and busyness.

I say all this primarily for focus; you don't have to pray for hours, just invite God, ask for the time together, and listen for how He leads you to pray. Prayer is a nonstop relationship with open communication both ways. Prayer is talking to your Best Friend, Your Creator who wants all of your dreams that He put in you, to come true.

The key to ecstasy is the posture of your heart, in your spirit, in prayer. It is not just in intimacy, it is an alignment that you actively try to maintain; yet, it is true that if you pray in the spirit during intimacy, God will open up new heights and levels of intimacy to you and your spouse that you never thought possible. God continues to blow my mind!

I firmly believe this is how God truly has created Love to be—pure, passionate, romantic, an intimacy that binds you deeper in the natural, but also deeper in the spiritual. *Ecstasy of Love* is possible—it is pure unadulterated Love in its truest form!

Appendix

REFERENCE STUDY

S CRIPTURE references appreciated from several translations. This is not a conclusive list; there are many more that are alluded to throughout the body of this work.

Introduction

1. Proverbs 23:7
2. John 14:26-27
3. Hebrews 11:1-6

Chapter 1 Pursing Excellence

4. Hebrews 4:12
5. Proverbs 29:18
6. Mark 9:23
7. Isaiah 55:8-9
8. Luke 12:34
9. Hebrews 13:5
10. Psalm 84:11
11. Psalm 51:17
12. Hebrews 10:25
13. Galatians 5:22-23
14. Matthew 18:19-20

Chapter 2 Defining Ecstasy

15. 1 Kings 18:12; 2 kings 2:12; Acts 8:39
16. John 20:19
17. Psalm 37:4
18. Job 22.28

Chapter 3 Fighting for Your Destiny

19. 1 Peter 5:8
20. Luke 22:31-32
21. Ecclesiastes 4:12
22. Exodus 20:14; Deuteronomy 5:18
23. John 10:10
24. Matthew 7:9; Luke 11:11
25. Matthew 5:8
26. Matthew 5:6.
27. Philippians 1:9-11
28. Colossians 1:27
29. James 4:7

Chapter 4 Two Ecstasy Killers

30. Romans 8:37
31. Luke 17:6; Matthew 17:20
32. Proverbs 3:5-6
33. 2 Chronicles 7:14

Chapter 5 Authentic Love

34. Isaiah 40:31
35. Romans 4:17
36. 1 Corinthians 2:7 AMP; Proverbs 25:2
37. Romans 8:28
38. 2 Corinthians 12:9
39. Isaiah 61: 7 AMP
40. Psalm 84:11

41. Isaiah 26:3

42. 1 Samuel 24 & 26:9; Chronicles 16:21-22; Psalm 105:11-15

43. Exodus 19:5; Deuteronomy 7:6

Chapter 6 Accept and Adapt

44. Psalm 139:7-10

45. Proverbs 14:12

46. Proverbs 19:13; 27:15

47. Psalm 37:23

Chapter 7 Always More!

48. 1 Corinthians 13:4-13 AMP

49. 1 Corinthians 10:23 NIV

50. 1John 4:18

51. Hebrews 13:5

52. Isaiah 43:19

53. 2 Corinthians 12:9

54. 1 Corinthians 13:13 AMP

55. Hebrews 11:6

56. James 2:17 NIV

Chapter 8 Ways to Encourage Ecstasy

57. Ephesians 4:26

58. John 15:5

59. Proverbs 3:6

60. Ephesians 5:21

61. Romans 13:1-7

62. Ephesians 5:22-24   1 Peter 3:1-5 AMP

63. Ephesians 5:28-29 AMP

64. 1 Peter 3:5-7 AMP

65. Ephesians 3:20 AMP

65. Proverbs 3:5-7

About the Author

S TEPHANIE Gossert is a passionate daughter of the King! Her zeal is contagious! She invokes desire to find the greater depth of life for which we were created. Stephanie encourages an equipping in all of the spiritual giftings. She believes our mandate, from the Lord as believers, is to *take the land*! Take the land inside ourselves, mind, body, and spirit; and also to *take and govern the land around us* as we are entrusted by the Lord. Stephanie has a strong conviction for us to not just be the Body of Christ, but for us to look like the Body of Christ! She believes it is time for us to be this nameless, faceless generation that does not need positions, titles, or pedestals to affirm the power of Christ that flows through us!

stephaniegossert@gmail.com.

About Shores of Grace

B ETWEEN the Flowers and the Broken are real life stories, songs, and lessons of how God moves through His people in healing in the streets of Brazil. Shores of Grace is a worship and missionary ministry currently headquartered in Recife, Brazil, led by Nic and Rachael Billman. The goal of our staff is to reveal Father God in all that we do. Whether we're leading worship in a church, walking the streets of Brazil or shopping at the local grocery store, we want to reveal the Father. This is the calling that God has placed on our lives and we believe it's a calling for the whole church, for all of the sons and daughters of the living God. To live a life of compassion and power where miracles and healing follow us everywhere we go, just as they did with Jesus.

This is a story where fact is harder to believe than fiction....

—Randy Clark, Global Awakening

I wept, rejoiced, pondered, and received as I read through this wonderful communication born of the Spirit.

—Patricia King, XPMedia

One night not long ago, Nic Billman and his team sat with a group of street children in Brazil. Passing around paper and crayons for them to draw with, Nic began to strum his guitar in worship. "Draw a picture of the Kingdom of God," he told the children. And as he sang, the children drew. At the end of the evening, as Nic looked through the pictures. The children had all drawn the same thing—a house. As he looked through the drawings Jesus quietly spoke to Nic's heart. "In my Father's house there are many rooms, and I go to prepare a place for you." What does the Kingdom of God look like to a little girl who sells her body for $3? What does the Kingdom of God look like to a little boy who ran from the violence at home to live on the streets? It looks like Daddy's house where He has prepared a place for them. All of creation is groaning and waiting for the revealing of the children of God—because through His children, the Father is revealed. He is calling us by name and inviting us to walk with Him through the garden of life—between the flowers and the broken—calling out to all, "Come home! The Father has prepared a place for you."

To get your copy of Between the Flowers and the Broken visit:
www.shoresofgrace.com

HOPE BIGLER

capturing life

www.hopebigler.com

South Central PA Boutique Photographer &
Destination Portrait Photographer